A SUBMARINERS' WAR

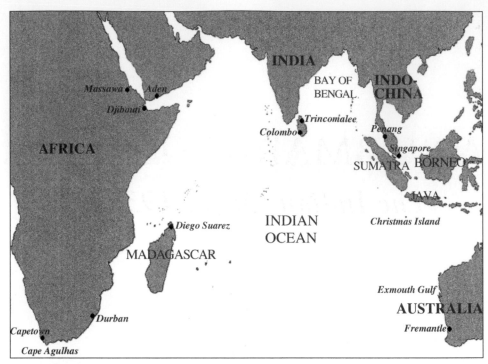

The Indian Ocean.

By the same author:

Baltic Assignment
Destination Dardanelles
Portrait of a Shipbuilder
(with Arnold Hague and Craig Carter)
Mediterranean Submarines, 1914-19
(with Paul Kemp)

A SUBMARINERS' WAR

The Indian Ocean 1939-45

Michael Wilson

TEMPUS

First published 2000

PUBLISHED IN THE UNITED KINGDOM BY:

Tempus Publishing Ltd
The Mill, Brimscombe Port
Stroud, Gloucestershire GL5 2QG

PUBLISHED IN THE UNITED STATES OF AMERICA BY:

Arcadia Publishing Inc.
A division of Tempus Publishing Inc.
2 Cumberland Street
Charleston, SC 29401
1-888-313-2665

Tempus books are available in France, Germany and Belgium
from the following addresses:

Tempus Publishing Group	Tempus Publishing Group	Tempus Publishing Group
21 Avenue de la République	Gustav-Adolf-Straße 3	Place de L'Alma 4/5
37300 Joué-lès-Tours	99084 Erfurt	1200 Brussels
FRANCE	GERMANY	BELGIUM

British Library Cataloguing in Publication Data.
A catalogue record for this book is available from the British Library.

ISBN 0 7524 2013 5

Typesetting and origination by Tempus Publishing.
PRINTED AND BOUND IN GREAT BRITAIN

For Yvonne
With my deepest love:
For her constant encouragement,
unfailing support and her always
invaluable common sense.

Le Vengeur *approaches a berth in Diego Suarez at the end of a patrol. (Admiral Francois)*

Silhouette of the Italian Submarine Cappellini.

Contents

ACKNOWLEDGEMENTS

It gives me great pleasure to acknowledge all the help that I have received from people in many countries while compiling this history.

Some historians and fellow authors have allowed me access to their material and given me permission to quote from their work. In particular I am grateful to *Capitaine de Vaisseau* Claude Huan, the author of *Les Sous-Marins Français 1919-45*; to Ian Trenowden, the author of *Operations Most Secret* and *Fighting Submarine*, who also kindly loaned me some photographs; to Commander Edward Young DSO DSC RNVR, the author of *One of Our Submarines*; to Arthur Banks, the author of *Wings of the Dawning*; to Bernard Edwards, the author of *Blood and Bushido*; and to John Beasant, the author of *Stalin's Silver*. I have quoted from *Dark Seas Above* by John Gibson; however, I regret that I have been unable to trace the publishers, the author or his heirs. I acknowledge my debt to them and apologise for any apparent lack of courtesy.

Several former submariners have taken the time to write to me with stories of their war. In particular I am grateful to Captain Lennox Napier DSO DSC RN who kindly gave me many details of the patrols of HMS *Olympus* in 1939 and 1940; also to Toshio Tanaka, who at one time served as the Navigating Officer of the submarine *I-166*; and to Satoru Terashima, who served in the base at Penang. Admiral Elio Sandoroni served as an officer in several submarines of the Italian East African flotilla and Monsieur François di Sotto served as a seaman in the Italian submarine *Perla*; both kindly wrote to me concerning the voyages made by the submarines from East Africa to Bordeaux in 1941.

Commander Jeff Tall MBE RN, the curator of the RN Submarine Museum at Gosport, has been most helpful in aiding my research, and Ms Debbie Corner has kindly helped with photographs from the Museum's extensive collection. I must record my sincere thanks to my good friend the late Gus Britton of the Submarine Museum who was, as ever, most helpful in sending me information and copies of some of his own photographs. I am grateful to Messrs David Brown, Bob Coopock, Arnold Hague and Alan Francis of the Naval Historical Branch of the Ministry of Defence in London for the help that they gave me when I first started off on the trail of this story.

I wish to express my thanks to Mr William Galvani, the Director of the Nautilus Memorial and Submarine Force Library and Museum in New London, and to Mr Bernard Cavalcante, the Head of the Operational Archives Branch of the Naval Historical Center in Washington, for their help in providing information concerning the patrol of the USS *Grenadier* off the coast of Malaya.

Mr C.F. Bruijn, of the Institute of Maritime History in the Ministry of Defence in The Hague, kindly provided documents and photographs concerning the activities of the Netherlands' submarines. Signor Mario Buracchia, of the Ufficio Storico della Marina Militare in Rome, was most helpful in answering my many questions and in providing me with photographs.

Captain Teruaki Kawano and Captain Noritaka Kitazawa of the National Institute for Defense Studies in Tokio gave me considerable assistance. I am grateful to Commander Kennosuke Torisu, the General Editor of *Nihon Kaigun Sensuikan Shi* (The History of Japanese Navy Submarines), and to Lieutenant Commander Tatsuo Tsukudo, later Vice-Admiral JMSDF, for their permission to use many of their photographs.

I am most grateful to Contrôleur Général des Armées Pierre-Yves Digard who kindly allowed me to use photographs taken by his father in 1940-41 when commanding the submarine *Le Vengeur*; and to Amiral François of the Association Générale Amicale des Anciens des Sous-Marins who has allowed me to use some of his personal photographs.

I wish to thank the following for their help: Frau Heike Altenpohl, the daughter of the late Horst Klatt, the only officer to survive the sinking of the *U-859*; Mr Michael Brassard; Dr Maurizio Brescia; Engineer Lieutenant Commander C. Cheffings (retd), who served in HMS *Kandahar* in 1940; Signora Liliana Giambarda, whose husband served in the submarine *Perla*; Monsieur Pierre Hérvieux; Herr Ottoheinrich Junker, the former Commanding Officer of the *U-*

532; Herr Frank Kaspras of the U-Boot *Kameradschaft*; Mr Paul Kemp; Mr Christopher Lowe; Herr Jürgen Oesten, the former Commanding Officer of the *U-861*; Herr Helmuth Pich, the former Commanding Officer of the *U-168*; Mr Norman Polmar; Herr Heinz Priesmier; Dr Achille Rastelli; Professor Dr Jurgen Rohwer; and Herr Heinz Trinkaus, who served as the German Paymaster in Penang.

Finally, I wish to record my very sincere thanks to Yvonne, my darling wife. Without her inspiration, encouragement and advice this book would never have been completed.

INTRODUCTION

During the First World War the Japanese had fought against the Germans on the side of the Allies, though once the Germans had been ousted from their Far Eastern Colonies early in the war there was little for the Japanese forces to do. However, they did send a destroyer flotilla to the Mediterranean to help protect merchant shipping from German and Austrian U-boats. During the 1930s their attitude began to change, more rapidly in the Army than in the Navy, but gradually the Japanese forces adopted a pro-German stance. The effect of this became more serious as the Army's influence in Japanese politics increased.

In a policy document dated October 1935 the British Chiefs of Staff stated: 'Our strategic plans in the Far East are based upon the possibilities of conflict with an increasingly powerful Japan.' Even so, they had to admit that they would be unable to fight a war in Europe and still hope to be prepared for a conflict with Japan. This was, however, precisely the situation in which they found themselves in 1939.

Japanese expansionism began with the occupation of Manchuria in 1931-32 and continued with the start of the war with China in 1937. The Japanese looked for increased concessions by the Dutch in the East Indies for the supply of oil, tin and rubber and became increasingly belligerent, particularly after the capture of the Netherlands by German forces in 1940. They realised that they faced comparatively little opposition to their plans when, after the Italian entry into the war in 1940, the British forces in the Far East were greatly reduced. Their worst fear was an attack by the Soviet Union, especially after the humiliating defeats of the Japanese Army by the Russians in 1938 and 1939. This fear was partly alleviated by the German-Soviet non-aggression pact of 1939, and then in 1941 the Japanese themselves signed a similar treaty with the Soviets.

By the summer of 1940 the Japanese controlled most of the coast of China but were unable to make further substantial advances in the interior. China received limited amounts of war material through Burma and through Indo-China. However, Britain acceded to Japanese demands to close the Burma Road, being unwilling to provoke the Japanese while fully committed to fighting the war alone against Germany. Similarly, the Vichy French promptly agreed to close the railway from Haiphong to Yunnan for movements of war supplies to the Chinese. No sooner had the French complied than the Japanese demanded the right to transport troops across the northern province of Tonkin and to build airfields in the region. The French appealed to the United States, who were in no position to give them any assistance other than to embargo shipments of certain strategic supplies to the Japanese. Consequently, a further agreement in September 1940 allowed the Japanese to station 6,000 troops in Tonkin, move troops along the railway into China and to use three airfields.

By the end of 1940, Thai – or Siamese, as they were then known – forces had began a series of local actions against the French in Indo-China over disputed areas of territory along the border. Fighting soon became widespread along most of the frontier. In January 1941 the French Navy inflicted a heavy defeat on the Thais at the battle of Koh-Chang. Japanese influence brought about a negotiated end to hostilities but left both sides subject to further Japanese intervention. This became apparent when, in July 1941, the Japanese humiliated the French even further and took over the whole colony, giving them bases much closer to Malaya and the Dutch East Indies. Admiral Jean Decroux, the Vichy Governor-General of Indo-China, tried to excuse this virtual occupation by claiming it was 'to defend the country against the de Gaullists, the Chinese and the British, whose troop concentrations (*sic*) in Malaya and Burma had led France and Japan to fear an Anglo-American attempt to occupy Indo-China.'

American attempts to curb further expansion by placing an embargo on an increasing number of goods, finally including the export of all oil to Japan and the freezing of Japanese assets, resulted in a rapid worsening of relations. This in turn led to the Japanese attack on Pearl Harbor and similar attacks against the British and the Dutch. The Japanese attacks on the Americans, at Pearl Harbor and in the Philippines, and on the British and the Dutch all occurred within a few hours of each other, though this is not readily apparent owing to the different time zones kept and the fact that the war at that time straddled the International Date Line. For example, the first landings in Malaya took place at 12.25 a.m. on 8 December (local time), an hour and a half *before* the air raid on Pearl Harbor at 8.00 a.m. on 7 December (local time). Reduced to a common time zone of GMT these times were 4.55 p.m. on the 7th and 6.30 p.m. on the 7th respectively.

The Japanese attack on Pearl Harbor not only surprised the Americans and the British but also Adolf Hitler. While talks were taking place in Berlin for a formal treaty of alliance with his Eastern partner, Hitler had been told only that war in the Far East was likely to come sooner than he expected, and the actual attack left him angry and slighted that the Japanese had not taken him into their confidence. It was a signal to the European partners in the Axis that the Japanese intended to fight the war in their own best interests without prior consultation with Berlin or Rome. Nevertheless Hitler and Mussolini fulfilled their pledge to declare war on the United States.

The story of the Battle of the Atlantic is well known. It was fought over many thousands of square miles of ocean and lasted until the German surrender in May 1945. The German U-boats tried – and failed, with horrendous losses – to stop the flow of men and supplies crossing from America to Britain. It was a battle which was crucial to the war in Europe, and had it been lost by Britain and her allies it would undoubtedly have meant that they lost the war. Similarly, the inability of the Germans to win the Battle of the Atlantic was greatly to reduce their hopes of winning the war.

Strangely, there was no Battle of the Pacific as such. The battle of attrition between the American and Japanese fleets, the subject of so much thought and planning by the admirals of both nations before the war, never took place. Thousands of ships crossed the Pacific in support of the American island-hopping campaigns almost unscathed by attack from Japanese submarines. It was a surprising omission by the Japanese Navy. In contrast, the American submarine force decimated the Japanese merchant navy.

The Indian Ocean provided another quite different scenario. Shipping between Australian or New Zealand ports and Britain or the Middle East had to cross its vast distances; tankers carrying the vital oil from the Persian Gulf had to pass the choke point from the Gulf into the Indian Ocean; India itself became the bastion where the British war effort against Japan was based. Despite the importance of the Indian Ocean to the Allies for much of the war, Axis activity in this area was limited and of relatively minor effectiveness. Initially the Italian submarines, based in East Africa, achieved nothing and when they later returned to the area it was as part of the German campaign. The German bases in France were far away and their submarines were required to spend months at sea if they were to patrol these waters. Later the Germans were allowed the use of Penang in Malaya as a forward base. The Japanese considered that their main effort was required in the Pacific and consequently sent relatively few submarines to operate in the Indian Ocean.

Nevertheless the Indian Ocean has one vital factor of interest to the submarine historian. It was the one area of the world where, uniquely, the submarines of seven nations – Great Britain, the Netherlands, the United States of America, France, Italy, Germany and Japan – all operated and fought during the war.

This then is the story of those submarine operations. It is not intended to be a detailed comprehensive chronology of who sank what and when, but rather a look at the overall picture of how the submarines were deployed and of the level of success they achieved.

Any attempt to define the limits of the Indian Ocean is complicated and often depends on the circumstances. For the purposes of this story the Indian Ocean includes the Red Sea, the Bay of Bengal and the Persian Gulf. To the west, the Ocean boundaries may be said to be the east coast of the African continent southward to Capetown and then due south; to the east, the boundary is the west coast of Australia northwards to Darwin, then across to the island of Timor, continuing along the northern coast of the Dutch East Indies and finally to Singapore. Operations in the South China Sea by the American and British submarine flotillas based in Fremantle do not form part of this story except in special circumstances where necessary.

One factor about the Indian Ocean that must not be forgotten is its vast size. It is the world's third largest ocean, covering approximately one-fifth of the total sea area of the world, and covers an area in excess of 28 million square miles. From Capetown to Singapore is 5,200 nautical miles (6,000 statute miles), to Colombo is 4,250 nautical miles (4,890 statute miles). For comparison, American submariners had to travel 1,200 miles from their main base at Pearl Harbor to Midway, where they could top up with fuel, with another 2,300 miles ahead of them before reaching their patrol billet off the Japanese coast; for those going down to Sydney there was a trip of 4,400 miles to be undertaken.

Since the events chronicled in this story the names of many places have changed. For example, Malaya has become Malaysia, Ceylon is Sri Lanka and the Dutch East Indies is now the independent state of Indonesia. As this is a story of the war years, the place names given are those which were in use at that time. Where there might be doubt, an explanation is given in the appropriate place.

One
The 'Phoney War'

In September 1938 Neville Chamberlain returned to London from his meeting with Adolf Hitler, waving his historic piece of paper and proclaiming 'peace in our time'. However, no one really shared his optimism and rearmament in Britain belatedly speeded up. Throughout the remainder of 1938 and into 1939 the spectre of a new European war increased. Mussolini's Italy was considered at best to be neutral but more likely to enter such a war on the side of Germany. The Royal Navy and its French ally would be fully occupied in countering the threat posed by the two Axis powers.

Meanwhile, the position which Japan would take in the event of a European war remained doubtful and a naval presence had to be maintained in the Far East to defend British interests should Japan decide to take advantage of the situation and Britain be forced to fight a war simultaneously on both sides of the world.

The Fourth Submarine Flotilla was based in Hong Kong and consisted of thirteen of the large 'O', 'P' and 'R' class submarines and two sister minelayers of the *Porpoise* class, the *Grampus* and *Rorqual*, and the depot ship HMS *Medway*. In the event of war with Japan it was intended that this flotilla would be the main force in holding up any Japanese seaborne attack on Malaya while waiting for reinforcements to arrive on station from Home Waters or the Mediterranean. This plan presupposed that reinforcements would actually be available and would not already be involved in a war nearer home. It is ironic that, by the time the Japanese did attack, this flotilla had been deployed elsewhere and seven of the fifteen submarines of the pre-war flotilla on the China Station had been lost.

Porpoise *class submarine like HMS* Grampus *and* Rorqual *of the 4th Submarine Flotilla and HMS* Seal *which was on passage to join them at the outbreak of war. The submarines of this class could carry fifty moored mines externally on rails running from*

forward to aft inside the submarine's casing. Note the periscopes offset to starboard to permit the mines to pass unhindered from forward to aft during a minelay.

The *Porpoise* class submarine HMS *Seal* (Lieutenant Commander Rupert Lonsdale) left Portsmouth on 4 August 1939 for Hong Kong, where she was to join the Fourth Submarine Flotilla. She was newly completed and the last of a class of six large minelaying submarines. When the Admiralty's War Telegram was received she was in Aden and was immediately sent on a patrol in the Straits of Bab el Mandeb at the southern end of the Red Sea. Her task was to intercept and stop any German merchant ships that were attempting to seek safety in the neutral harbours of Italian East Africa.

No German ships were seen on that or a subsequent patrol; however, an excited British tanker, believing the *Seal* to be a U-boat, tried – and fortunately failed – to ram her. The *Seal* was then sent to Alexandria for stores and additional torpedoes, but instead of returning home as was expected she was sent back to Aden. These orders were cancelled when she was half way down the Red Sea and by mid-October the *Seal* was back where she had started in August, in Portsmouth.

These patrols served to illustrate some of the difficulties faced by submarines when intercepting merchant ships in the early days of the war. Peacetime training had been directed solely towards an attack on enemy warships and submarine warfare against trade had hardly been considered, yet once war was declared many submarines were sent out to intercept enemy merchant ships. While carrying out this task they were expected to act in accordance with the detailed rules laid down by the Admiralty in a book called *The Prize Manual* – but this book was not issued to submarines until the end of 1939!

The Prize Manual was in some instances even more restrictive than International Law. The Commanding Officer of any British warship was instructed that if he stopped a merchant ship then that ship was to be boarded and searched for contraband. If the vessel was enemy owned or carrying contraband then it could be taken in as a prize. Only as a last resort, and then only if the safety of the crew could be ensured, could the ship be sunk. Even for a warship like a destroyer this was by no means likely to be an easy task, but a submarine had no way of putting a prize crew onboard a suspect merchant ship, and in any case had no crew to spare for such a purpose. How could a submarine's Commanding Officer ensure the safety of an enemy crew? There was no room in the submarine for them, and placing the enemy crew in open boats out of sight of land was not considered acceptable as a means of ensuring their safety.

One is left wondering just what Lonsdale and other submarine Commanding Officers were expected to do in these circumstances. At least Lonsdale, in the waters off Aden, would not have been worried about having to be on the surface in daylight with the risk of being surprised by an enemy aircraft. This was just one more worry for those submarines operating in enemy waters – like the *Salmon*, when in the approaches to the Skagerrak in December 1939. With the large liner

Bremen passing within a mile as she headed back to Germany at speed, the *Salmon* surfaced and ordered the German vessel to stop. However, the *Bremen* steamed on, and a German aircraft forced the submarine to dive before she had the chance to enforce her order. How the rules were to change as the war progressed.

As late as 26 June 1939 the Committee of Imperial Defence in London considered reinforcing the submarine flotilla in the Far East, but this was impossible since the Admiralty had few enough boats in Home Waters as war with Germany became more and more of a probability. As the international situation deteriorated, eight submarines of the flotilla, including the two minelayers, left Hong Kong with the *Medway* on 11 August for Singapore as part of a prearranged peacetime cruise. By the 19th the situation was sufficiently serious for the Commander-in-Chief, Admiral Sir Geoffrey Layton, himself a famous submariner of the previous war, to consider deploying his forces to counter any moves by Japan should she elect to side with Germany. Apart from the operational submarines at Singapore he had four more in Hong Kong which would be ready within a week. A further two submarines were refitting in Hong Kong and one in Singapore.

Also arriving in Singapore at this time was *L'Espoir*, the only French submarine then based at Saigon in Indo-China.[1] The original intention had been that she would work with the British submarines from Singapore on the outbreak of war, but in the event *L'Espoir* returned to Saigon on 1 September and subsequently sailed for coastal surveillance of the French colony, the French having even less optimism than their British allies regarding the intentions of the Japanese.

By the outbreak of war in Europe the submarine patrols were in position, their task made easier by the fact that the Foreign Office in London considered it had become more likely that Japan would remain neutral – for the time being at least. The aim of these patrols was twofold; firstly, to sink any German ship specified by the Admiralty as a raider and secondly, to intercept any of the enemy's merchant ships trying to make for a friendly port, particularly in Japan or Soviet Russia. The threat from raiders disguised as merchant ships was no idle one. At the outbreak of war there were some forty German merchant vessels in the area, many of which were considered suitable for conversion. From Singapore the submarines went to areas off the Sunda Strait and Sabang in northern Sumatra, and within the Malacca Strait off the Sumatran port of Belawan Deli to the west of Penang. The submarines which had remained in Hong Kong went on patrol between Formosa (now Taiwan) and the Phillipines.

The submarine Commanding Officers were concerned by what precise action they would be expected to take should they meet with the enemy, so much so that one broke radio silence to ask for guidance. Captain (S) Four, Captain G.M.K. Keble White in the *Medway*, replied: 'Report not attack'. The Commander-in-Chief confirmed this decision and referred Commanding Officers to *The Prize*

Manual, seemingly oblivious to the fact that the book was not then carried on board submarines. Amidst all the doubt and confusion the one fact that was firmly established was that Dutch territorial waters in the East Indies, now Indonesia, were not to be infringed at any time.

With the German pocket battleship *Graf Spee* at large in the South Atlantic and possibly about to break through to the Indian Ocean, an additional patrol was instituted in the Lombok Straits. On 24 October four of the 'O' class submarines were detached to the East Indies Fleet to form the 8th Submarine Flotilla based at Colombo in Ceylon (now Sri Lanka). The rest of the submarines of the 4th Flotilla remained east of Singapore and their actions form no further part of this story, although they continued to carry out numerous surveillance patrols in areas as diverse as the Dutch East Indies in the south to the Russian port of Vladivostok in the north for the remainder of their time in the Far East, after which they transferred to the Mediterranean.

Joining the submarines of the new 8th Flotilla was the old depot ship *Lucia*. She was then thirty-two years old, having been built in 1907 in West Hartlepool for the German *Hamburg-Amerika* line. She was captured as a prize near the West Indian island of St Lucia in 1914 and after a period with the Elder Dempster line she was acquired by the Admiralty in 1916 and converted for use as submarine depot ship, a task she carried out until replaced by the newly built *Forth* in early 1939. She was sent out to Bombay to be placed in reserve, and was re-commissioned at the outbreak of war and sent to Masirah for convoy duties until the submariners required her services again.

The *Graf Spee* had left Germany before the outbreak of war. The raider's first victim, the 5,000 ton British liner *Clement*, was not sunk until 30 September 1939. After sinking several other vessels in the South Atlantic, *Kapitän zur See* Hans Langsdorff took the ship on a wide sweep round the Cape of Good Hope, passing about 400 miles south of Cape Agulhas, and by 10 November was 200 miles south of Madagascar. The suggestion that he might have approached the virtually defenceless South African coast in order to bombard shipping and oil installations ignores the specific instructions given to Langsdorff before sailing, which stated that he was not to endanger his ship by operating in areas where the Royal Navy might be met. His short inroad into the Indian Ocean was merely a diversion to confuse the many forces which were hunting the German ship.

The ship's presence in the Indian Ocean was revealed on 15 November when she sank the small tanker *Africa Shell*, 706 tons, 160 miles north-east of Lourenco Marques and 10 miles off the African coast. The British crew were released and the next day the *Graf Spee* again advertised her presence by stopping the neutral Dutch ship *Mapia* in the same area. The battleship then left the Indian Ocean, again passing well to the south of Cape Agulhas.

However, the British continued to fear that the *Graf Spee* might operate in the

Indian Ocean against Allied merchant shipping, as had been done so successfully by German raiders in 1914. There were a large number of sheltered anchorages in the many remote islands of the area which could be used by a raider to rest up and carry out essential maintenance. The same islands could be used by German supply ships which might be waiting to service the battleship. It was to some of these areas that the submarines of the new Flotilla were now sent.

In early November two patrols were instituted for the Colombo-based submarines. The first, which was expected to last a month and became known as the 'short' patrol, was to the Chagos Archipelago and the Maldive Islands. The second, giving the submarine two months away and known as the 'long' patrol, was to the Seychelles area. Submarines on both patrols were required to search out the many islands in their areas for any signs of German activity.

HMS *Otus* and *Odin* were the first to sail, leaving Colombo in early November for the Chagos Islands. By the time the *Otus* returned on 5 December she had steamed nearly 3,900 (nautical) miles, mostly on the surface, and had seen no signs of the Germans.[2] Indeed, when she had arrived off a small group known as 'Six Islands' the local population thought this was the arrival of a German U-boat and that they would probably be killed. The fact that the first submarine they had ever seen was British rather than German had, as the Commanding Officer wrote in his report,[3] 'a great morale effect'.

HMS *Odin* had an equally fruitless patrol in December, hampered by a heavy westerly or north-westerly swell which made conditions onboard very uncomfortable. The Engine Room staff, led by the indefatigable Warrant Engineer G.H. Cook, had to deal with a defective engine clutch which took fifty-eight hours to repair, with the submarine rolling constantly the whole time. During this patrol a large number of ratings suffered from outbreaks of boils brought on by the heat and high humidity. One rating with a temperature of 104°F was treated for a liver condition by the *Infirmier* on Diego Garcia and again by a doctor from the RFA *Olna*, but he remained ill for the remainder of the patrol. On return to Colombo Lieutenant Commander R.W. Moir reported[4] that the only suitable anchorages which a raider could use to fuel and provision quickly were at Peros Banhos and Diego Garcia. There had been no sign of the Germans at either place. The Chagos Bank provided no suitable anchorage in the prevailing weather conditions, which were liable to last until March.

The 'long patrol' of HMS *Olympus* (Commander H.V. King) is perhaps the most remarkable non-operational patrol carried out by a British submarine during the course of the war. She had sailed from Colombo for the Seychelles on 17 November and it was while she was on passage to her area that news came through of the sinking of the *Africa Shell* on the 15th. It was decided that the *Otus* and *Odin* should remain in the Chagos Islands which were some 2,500 miles away from this area, but the *Olympus* would be diverted to the Mozambique Channel.

HMS Otus, *a pre-war picture. The* Otus *was completed in 1929 and scrapped in 1946. The 4-inch gun in this class is mounted at the forward end of the conning tower above the level of the casing. (RN Submarine Museum)*

As is now known, the *Graf Spee* had quickly doubled back into the Atlantic and it is therefore not surprising that the British submarines spent fruitless days searching in vain for the German battleship.

The *Olympus* was then sent to the French base of Diego Suarez in Madagascar to top up with fuel and fresh food. It was not a happy visit. Lieutenant Lennox Napier, the submarine's First Lieutenant, recalls[5] that the combination of heat, flies, lack of shore amenities and dockyard inefficiency made their time in harbour unpleasant. The French dockyard Commandant held the view that life for French soldiers in the Maginot line was extremely disagreeable and it was, therefore, the duty of French forces elsewhere to lead an equally miserable existence – and this also applied to any ally who visited the French base. It is reported that such austere measures even extended to French civilians living in the base, who were forbidden to play the gramophone in their own homes!

On 19 December the Commander-in-Chief, East Indies, received information that D/F [Direction Finding] bearings of a signal placed an enemy unit near Prince Edward Island, 1,200 miles south-east of the South African coast. The *Olympus* at Diego Suarez was the nearest Allied warship; even so, she was over 2,000 miles from the island. Nevertheless she was ordered to proceed 'with all despatch' to intercept. What this order overlooked was the fact that the *Olympus* was stored and kitted out for a tropical patrol and Prince Edward Island was 1,200 miles south-east of Capetown in latitude 47° South – in the path of the Roaring Forties. There was no warm clothing onboard and charts and Sailing Directions had to be extracted, not without great difficulty, from the French. The navigational information was outdated but did promise, truthfully, 'coups de vent formidables'. Sufficent material was obtained to make just four sets of canvas protective clothing for the use of the bridge personnel.[6] After taking on fuel and lubricating oil the submarine sailed.

Just how D/F bearings of an enemy vessel could have placed it in the vicinity of Prince Edward Island at that time is not clear. It is certain that neither of the two islands of the group were hosting the enemy, for their inhospitable shores offered no suitable anchorage. Whatever the facts, it was to these isolated islands that the *Olympus* was sent. They were uninhabited, volcanic in origin and from the unbroken coastline steep escarpments rose to rugged peaks.

In these lonely waters Commander King soon found that the lubricating oil provided by the French was of the wrong specification, and the submarine's engines broke down frequently. As the submarine moved south the temperature dropped over fifty degrees in a week, from 89°F to 33°F. To add to the misery of all onboard the wind reached Force 11, and in mountainous seas the bridge watchkeepers suffered in their inadequate protective clothing, already soaked through from days of use. A night watch for icebergs was kept on the Asdic (now known as Sonar); despite the prevailing conditions their presence was detected in time for avoiding action to be taken. After leaving Diego Suarez the submarine was ordered to investigate the Crozet Islands, another group of uninhabited volcanic islands situated to the east of Prince Edward Island.

As the submarine approached the islands one engine failed. In sight of the bleak towering cliffs which rose to 6,500 feet in the centre of the Isle de la Possession, with gigantic waves breaking at their base, the second engine failed. By heroic efforts the Engine Room staff got one engine to start again and the submarine clawed its way back from the inhospitable shore which obviously provided no shelter for any ship, enemy or otherwise. Commander King, no doubt with considerable relief, then left the area. After a look at Prince Edward Island the *Olympus* headed for Durban, her passage marked by the continual failure of first one engine and then the other; it was a rare occurrence for both to be going at the same time. During this time Christmas came and went almost unnoticed by the crew in the midst of their troubles.

As the submarine neared Durban the order came to remain on the surface and act as a target for a search exercise by the South African Air Force. The exercise was very useful for the airmen but the submariners were somewhat aggrieved that no one had told them that the SAAF were equipped with German aircraft!

HMS Olympus *in Malta in early 1941. In June 1942 the* Olympus *brought stores and petrol to Malta but was mined and sunk on the return passage. (Paul Kemp)*

The *Olympus* reached Durban on 29 December and went into the dockyard for repairs. By 22 January 1940 she was back in Colombo, having travelled over 12,000 miles. In his report Commander King[7] stated that: 'Prince Edward Island and Crozet Island were unlikely refuges for enemy raiders or supply ships, owing to lack of suitable sheltered anchorages and extremely inclement weather.' It was such a statement of the obvious that it seems incredible that these facts had to be obtained by sending a submarine to investigate. Commander King later received the OBE for this patrol, but before then he had been relieved and the *Olympus* had a new Captain.

Despite the fact that the pocket battleship *Graf Spee* had been sunk off Montevideo in early December, the patrols continued in the expectation that a German raider or supply ship might be met. The *Otus* went back to the Seychelles in the New Year and returned to Colombo on 1 March. The *Odin* also patrolled in the Chagos area.

The *Olympus* and *Orpheus* were sent out to cover the passage of a large convoy taking the first Australian and New Zealand troops to the Middle East. Starting near Chagos they worked up through the islands towards the track of the convoy. Finally, on the night of 1/2 February, they had the satisfaction of remaining unseen whilst they watched the twelve large liners packed with troops pass safely through the Nine Degree Channel.

As with all the other patrols carried out by the 8th Flotilla submarines during these months, there was always the chance that the Germans might be met at any time in the vicinity of one or other of the islands. Nevertheless the crews considered the task to be most unwarlike and for the most part it was simply a series of cruises among beautiful coral atolls which in those days were rarely visited by outsiders. Their principal concern was the heat, which affected everyone onboard and made the prospect of a bridge watch much appreciated.

Lieutenant Napier recalls[8] the *Olympus* visiting a low-lying coral island, appropriately named on the chart as Danger Island. It was obvious that no ship, friendly or otherwise, was present and there were large areas on the chart where no soundings were shown. Approaching too close, the submarine inevitably came to a halt on the coral reef, but fortunately was undamaged. Getting off the reef was quite easy but regaining the open sea was a different matter as they continued to bump into the coral heads that covered the lagoon. Eventually Napier was sent to lie prone in the bows from where it was possible to see the coral in the crystal clear water. At dead slow speed and 'employing the hand signals of a demented car-driver' he was able to direct the Captain in manoeuvring the submarine clear.

On another occasion the submarine visited an island where the local headman announced his intention of honouring the visitors with the gift of a live turtle. It was a large animal and quite impossible to take onboard so the islanders decided to kill it and give the carcass to the Captain to make turtle soup. The unfortunate turtle was a female and found to contain at least a gross of unlaid eggs which were reputed to be good eating. As neither the cook nor the Chinese stewards (still onboard as a relic of peacetime) were able to make the soup, the First Lieutenant wanted to throw the lot overboard as soon as they were clear of the islands. The Captain vetoed this idea as wasteful, but he was the only one to try the eggs as part of his breakfast. Eventually the First Lieutenant arranged for the bloody mess of turtle pieces and eggs to be thrown overboard while the Captain was sleeping, as the crew were unable to stomach their presence any longer and the glassy stare of the animal's head proved rather disconcerting.

In March 1940 events in Europe dictated the movements of the submarines based in Colombo and Singapore. Tension was mounting as the Italians became increasingly likely to enter the war on the side of the Germans, and the submarines were required in the Mediterranean. The two on patrol went direct to Aden and thence to Alexandria. The other two joined up with the depot ship HMS *Medway* and the five submarines from the China Station when they passed through Colombo in April. They all reached Alexandria in the middle of May. The remaining five submarines in Singapore sailed individually for the Mediterranean once they had completed their refits. The last to leave, on 22 August, was HMS *Rover* which, despite having to pass the then enemy held coast of the southern Red Sea, reached Alexandria in safety. Ironically, the *Rover* was back in the dockyard at Singapore when the Japanese attacked in December 1941.

There were then no British submarines in the Indian Ocean. The first phase of the war in those waters was over; none of the submarines had seen any action, indeed they had not even sighted the enemy.

Notes:

1 A second French submarine, *Le Phénix*, had sunk off Cam Ranh Bay in Indo-China in June 1939 after a battery explosion. See Chapter Three.

2 Report of Proceedings held in the Public Record Office (PRO) under reference ADM199/1831.

3 *ibid*.

4 HMS *Odin* Report of Proceedings ADM1/17304.

5 Private letter from Captain Lennox Napier DSO DSC RN to the author with many details of this patrol.

6 *History of Submarine Operations Vol.III*, reference ADM234/382.

7 ADM199/1831 and ADM199/300.

8 Captain Napier's letter to author.

Two
The Italians

6 September 1940: Britain and her Empire had been at war with Germany for a year and with Italy for nearly three months. France, Britain's ally, had been defeated and was largely occupied by her enemies; her Empire was split, part being loyal to the Government in Vichy, the remainder loyal to General de Gaulle in London. On that day, off the coast of Africa, convoy BN4 was sailing sedately up the Red Sea towards its destination at Sucz. Nineteen ships had sailed from Karachi and Bombay, and as the convoy passed the port of Aden five ships had detached with their cargoes of troops and, strangely, camels to reinforce the garrison. At the same time another eighteen ships had joined the convoy, taking more troops, fuel and the necessities of war to the army in Egypt.[1] The sole escort was the cruiser HMS *Leander*, reflecting concern for the safety of the ships in the convoy should they come under attack by the Italian destroyers based in the Eritrean port of Massawa. With the Saudi and Yemeni coasts over to starboard and the enemy coast to port there was no scope for evasion, and 150 miles was little enough distance for the seven fast Italian destroyers to travel.

Massawa was also the base for the Italian submarines, but no anti-submarine escort had been provided for the convoy. This was partly due to a shortage of escorts in the area and partly from an appreciation that the submarines would be unlikely to attack in waters so restricted by natural geography and underwater obstacles. In the weeks since the outbreak of war with Italy her East African based submarines had been without any significant successes and after the first few days of war had rarely posed a threat.

One ship was missing from the convoy that afternoon. The small Greek tanker *Atlas*, of some 4,000 tons, had dropped well astern of the convoy and was officially

The Italian submarine Luigi Settembrini *in the floating dock at Massawa in 1935. Note the four stern tubes. The* Luigi Settembrini *was not in East Africa when Italy entered the war, having returned to Italy in 1938, but the photograph serves to illustrate the size of the Italian ocean-going submarines. After the Italian surrender in 1943 the* Luigi Settembrini *was used for anti-submarine training by Allied forces and was then accidentally rammed and sunk by an American destroyer in the Atlantic in November 1944. (Ufficio Storico della Marina Militaire, Rome)*

classed as a 'straggler'. One Italian submarine was also at sea in the area, the *Guglielmotti*. Her Commanding Officer, *Capitano di Corvetta* Carlo Tucci, had failed to sight the convoy as it passed earlier but he had spotted the lonely Greek tanker. At six knots the *Atlas* was an easy target and Tucci did not miss with his torpedoes.[2] The tanker soon sank, leaving thirty survivors in the water to be picked up later in the day by the destroyer HMS *Kimberley*.

This was not an auspicious attack, but then this was not a war in which the Italian submarines of the Red Sea Flotilla had distinguished themselves. The *Atlas* was only their second success against merchant shipping in three months – and was destined to be the last.

When hostilities began in September 1939 between Germany, Italy's ally, and

Britain and France, there were already eight Italian submarines based in East Africa: the *Argo, Valella, Otaria, Glauco, Brin, Berillo, Onice* and *Iride*. Some of these had seen active service in the Mediterranean during the Spanish Civil War; indeed, the *Onice* and the *Iride* had actually served with their Italian crews under the Spanish flag of General Franco's Nationalist forces for some months. By the summer of 1939 all were badly in need of a refit. The *Glauco* returned to Home Waters at the end of 1939; then, in the spring of 1940, the remainder – with the exception of the *Onice* and *Iride* – also returned and were replaced by the *Archimede, Galileo Galilei, Ferraris, Guglielmotti, Perla* and *Macalle*. Finally, just prior to Italy's entry into the war, the two coastal submarines, the *Onice* and *Iride*, were replaced by the ocean-going *Torricelli* and *Luigi Galvani*.[3] As ships, albeit warships, of a neutral nation all the submarines had passed openly through the Suez Canal on their way to and from their bases in Italy. Thus, when war broke out between Italy and Great Britain in June 1940 the Italians had eight submarines based in Massawa along with seven destroyers and a small number of other ships.

It is remarkable that Mussolini had allocated this surprisingly small squadron to Massawa for such vital operations in the Red Sea. The Italian Navy was the third largest in Europe, with more cruisers than the combined British and French Mediterranean fleets, and the presence of just a few of these, together with a few more from their large submarine fleet of over 100 vessels, would surely have made a more effective contribution to his dreams of conquest. As it was, British convoys with stores and troop reinforcements sailed with virtual impunity in the Indian Ocean and up the Red Sea to Egypt, save only for minor losses such as occurred within Convoy BN4.

The Red Sea itself presented the Italian submariners with the navigational problem of operating in confined and dangerous waters beset with reefs. There was, however, plenty of open water nearby and the six large ocean-going submarines had sufficient range to have posed a threat at focal points such as the approaches to the Persian Gulf or even off Durban. As early as the end of April 1940 the [British] Admiralty had diverted all but the fastest merchant ships away from the Mediterranean, ordering them to go around the Cape because of fears of a declaration of war by Italy. The large Italian submarines, refuelling in Mogadishu in Italian Somaliland, could have reached the area off Durban and caused considerable damage as there were no anti-submarine forces in that area. The two smaller submarines would have been able to cover the ports of Aden and Djibouti.

The climate also presented problems, as the submarines were forced to operate in adverse conditions of high temperatures and, at that time of year, high humidity. Temperatures of over 100°F were frequently reported when dived. Worse still, most of the boats were having trouble with their air-conditioning plants which could, and did, give off poisonous methyl chloride gas.

The Archimede *leaving Taranto for the Red Sea in early 1940 before Italy's entry into the war. (Ufficio Storico della Marina Militaire, Rome)*

Although Italian East Africa was isolated from the rest of the Italian Empire there were ample stocks of ammunition and fuel in Massawa at the outbreak of war. However, there would be no chance of replacing them until the time came when the weak British forces in the Sudan and Egypt could be defeated and a link made with the Italians advancing into Egypt from Libya. In June 1940 British intelligence sources in London believed that there were only sufficient stocks of fuel in East Africa for five months. In the event, vast stocks were found in captured territory long after that period had elapsed, to say nothing of the fuel destroyed by the RAF in bombing raids or by the retreating Italians themselves. One source states that there were 20,000 tons of fuel for submarines,[4] clearly sufficient for many patrols when the larger boats had a capacity of about 90 tons each.

As soon as war was declared by Mussolini in June 1940 the submarines *Ferraris, Luigi Galvani, Galileo Galilei* and *Maccale* had all sailed from Massawa to carry out attacks on British and French shipping.[5] Of these four, only the *Ferraris* had returned safely, but then she had only stayed at sea for three days. She had been sent to patrol off the French port of Djibouti but suffered with battery trouble, making it impossible for her to remain at sea. She was back in Massawa by 14 June, being replaced on patrol by the *Torricelli*.

The first Italian submarine to be lost was the *Macalle*, one of a large class of short range submarines of about 700 tons surface displacement and just under 200 feet in length. They were known as 'The Africans' as they were all named after places in the Italian African colonies. Each submarine was armed with six 533mm (21 inch) torpedo tubes, of which four were forward and two aft; a spare reload torpedo was carried for each tube. There was also a 100mm (3.9 inch) deck gun with some extra bridge mounted machine guns. The maximum surface speed was 14 knots, $7\frac{1}{2}$ knots while dived.

Sent to patrol off Port Sudan, the *Macalle* was in trouble almost from the moment she left Massawa.[6] Many of the crew were affected by fever, pains, fits of vomiting and cramp, almost certainly brought on by leaks of gas from the air-conditioning system. Rough weather added to the distress of those who suffered from sea-sickness, with the boat rolling even when dived at a depth of about 60 feet, an experience not normally encountered by submariners. One Petty Officer was so ill that he could barely stand. Then, shortly after two o'clock on the morning of the 15th, the *Macalle* ran aground while on the surface charging her

The Archimede *and* Torricelli *in Massawa before the outbreak of war. (Ufficio Storico della Marina Militaire, Rome)*

31

batteries. No one was hurt but the submarine rapidly heeled over to port to an alarming degree, water started to flood in and chlorine was given off from the batteries. The Commanding Officer, *Tenente di Vascello* Alfredo Morone, had no alternative but to order everyone on deck.

Daylight found them in a difficult position. The submarine was firmly aground on her beam ends and filling with water. A short distance away lay the small island of Barra Musa, deserted and waterless. By evening everyone had reached the islet with all the stores that could be salvaged from the submarine. Using a small dinghy they were able to take ashore a limited amount of provisions and water. As the last of the crew was leaving, the bows of the submarine slowly rose into the air as she slipped off the reef and disappeared from sight, leaving only some flotsam and an oil slick to show she had ever been there.

It was obvious that with their pitifully limited resources they would be unable to survive for long. They needed urgent rescue. That night three men, with an *Aspirante* (Midshipman) in command, set off in the dinghy to get help. They had the choice of going to Port Sudan, about 30 miles to the north, or considerably further to the Eritrean coast to the south. They chose the latter course, mainly because of the thought of reaching friendly territory. It took the small boat and its crew three days to arrive at Bas Kasar nearly 100 miles away. They subsequently managed to reach a Frontier Post from where they were able to send a message to Massawa for help.

On Barra Musa the remainder of the crew suffered from thirst and hunger which exacerbated the exhaustion and sickness which had preceded the boat's grounding. They tried, not very successfully, to distil their own water, raided some birds' nests for the eggs and caught a few fish, but this did little to ease their pangs. One man died.

Early on the 22nd a British reconnaissance aircraft sighted a wrecked submarine lying in the clear water and then the survivors on their barren island. As a result the authorities in Port Sudan proposed to send an armed party in a tug – the only vessel available – to the area to take them off.[7] Before the tug could reach the Italians, help of a different kind had arrived. Soon after the British aircraft had departed, the crew of the *Macalle* were delighted to see a submarine approaching, although there were initial fears that it might perhaps be British. It was the *Guglielmotti*. When the British party arrived later in the day the island was deserted once more, with few signs of the drama that had taken place there.

The *Galileo Galilei* (*Capitano di Corvetta* Corrado Nardi) also sailed from Massawa on the outbreak of war to patrol the approaches of the port of Aden. She was considerably larger than the *Macalle*: 231 feet overall and displacing nearly 1,000 tons on the surface and 1,259 tons when dived. She was armed with eight 530mm torpedo tubes and had two 100mm (3.9 inch) deck guns. She had a maximum surface speed of 17 knots and a range of over 10,000 miles at eight knots.

On 16 June the *Galileo Galilei* stopped the Norwegian tanker *James Stove* about ten miles south of Aden. Nardi gave the crew fifteen minutes to abandon ship before firing the torpedoes which gave the Italian submarine its first, and only, victim. The flames from the sinking ship were seen by the trawler *Moonstone* (Boatswain W.J.M. Moorman), which hastened to the scene and rescued the crew from the boats. The armed boarding steamer *Chantala* was also in the area and actually saw the submarine before it dived, but was unable to follow up the contact as she was not fitted with Asdics.

Two days later Nardi stopped the Jugoslav steamer *Drava* by firing a couple of rounds from the forward 100mm gun across the bows. As the *Drava* belonged to a neutral state and was not carrying cargo of use to the Allied war effort she was released and allowed to go on her way, but the sound of gunfire had been heard ashore and an RAF fighter aircraft – an obsolete Gloster Gladiator – had been sent out to investigate. The fighter shadowed the submarine until a bomber arrived from Aden, only about twenty-six miles away. Three bombs were dropped which fell wide to one side before the submarine dived.

The destroyer *Kandahar* and the sloop *Shoreham* were next to arrive on the scene but it was dark before the search started. In the meantime the *Galileo Galilei* had surfaced again and tried to use its radio to send a message to Massawa. The destroyer immediately detected this and contact was gained before the submarine dived. The *Shoreham* managed to make two attacks with depth charges but they were not close enough to damage the submarine and both ships subsequently lost contact.

The submarine surfaced briefly during the night and again attempted to use her radio. A dawn search by RAF Blenheim aircraft from Aden failed to locate the submarine in the monsoon weather. Shortly before noon the trawler *Moonstone* gained a firm contact on Asdic at 5,000 yards and attacked with just one depth charge set to explode at 150 feet. A full pattern could not be risked as the ship's speed against the swell was too slow. Two more similar attacks were made. Four minutes after the second, Boatswain Moorman was surprised to see the submarine surface about a mile astern.

The submarine opened fire with her deck guns as the *Moonstone* altered course towards her. In turn, the *Moonstone* opened fire with her ancient 4 inch gun. The Italian gunners fired only a few erratic rounds before they were driven from their position by fierce but well directed bursts from the trawler's Lewis gun, enthusiastically assisted by every spare hand who could use a rifle. As the trawler remained bows on to her more powerful opponent the British gunners soon began to hit the submarine, first gaining a direct hit at the base of the conning tower and then another at the top which finished the action. The submarine crew

The Galileo Galilei *moored in Aden harbour after capture. The stern of a destroyer, probably* HMS Kandahar, *can be seen lying ahead of the submarine. The submarine was later commissioned as HMS X2 and briefly used for training. The name was changed again later in the war to the* P711. *(Lieutenant Commander Cheffings)*

began rushing on deck, waving bits of white cloth and hauling down the boat's ensign. The little *Moonstone* had achieved the unbelievable and captured an enemy submarine.[8]

The *Kandahar* then arrived opportunely on the scene and put a Prize Crew onboard before rescuing the demoralised Italians. Attempts to tow the submarine in the heavy monsoon swell proved unsuccessful, but it was found possible to start the submarine's own engines for the short passage back to port. In this manner the submarine was brought into Aden escorted by a proud Boatswain Moorman and his crew in the *Moonstone*.

In the aftermath Boatswain Moorman was awarded the Distinguished Service Cross, and others of his crew were also decorated. The *Galileo Galilei* was repaired and commissioned into the Royal Navy as HMS *X2*, where she had a short and inglorious career as a training target before being scrapped in 1946. More importantly, papers found onboard indicated that another Italian submarine had sailed from Massawa at the same time and was then on patrol in the approaches to the Gulf of Oman.

The *Luigi Galvani* (*Capitano di Corvetta* Renato Spano) was indeed on patrol in the focal area of the approaches to the Persian Gulf and, in the early hours of 23 June, torpedoed the Indian Navy sloop *Pathan*. As a result of the information gathered from the *Moonstone's* prize, the sloop HMS *Falmouth* and the destroyer

HMS *Kimberley* were diverted to the Gulf of Oman. The *Falmouth* gained contact shortly after reaching the area at about 11 p.m. on the 23rd when a darkened object was sighted by moonlight, fine on the port bow at a range of about 2½ miles. It was identified as a surfaced submarine steaming slowly, probably charging its batteries.

The *Falmouth* approached to about 600 yards before she challenged the submarine and, receiving no reply, opened fire with her forward 4 inch gun. The third round scored a direct hit aft of the conning tower but the flash of the gun prevented details from being seen. The submarine immediately began to dive and moved rapidly across the sloop's bow with only the conning tower visible. The *Falmouth* turned to ram as she closed in on the submarine. Fortunately for the *Falmouth* the submarine was too deep to be hit fatally and the sloop struck only a glancing blow, causing no damage to herself and serving only to push the submarine down even deeper. At this point she dropped three depth charges, two set to explode at 100 feet and one at 150 feet.

The resultant explosions sandwiched the *Luigi Glavani* and blew her to the surface again. First the bow appeared at a steep angle, then she righted herself and seemed to settle on an even keel with conning tower and casing clear of the water. As the crew began to emerge on deck waving white clothing the submarine began to lose trim and she sank by the stern. Three officers and twenty-seven ratings were picked up by the *Kimberley*, which had joined her consort; the remainder of the crew were lost, either going down with their boat or drowning before help could reach them.[9]

In fact the *Falmouth* had not been sighted until she made the challenge. Her first round had fallen short but had then ricocheted through the conning tower, killing the coxswain. The third round, the one seen to have hit, pierced the pressure hull and exploded in the motor room. The boat was rapidly filling with water when the depth charges went off and it is ironic that without their help the submarine might never have reached the surface at all.

The *Torricelli* (*Capitano di Corvetta* Salvatore Pelosi) had been sent to patrol off Djibouti when the *Ferraris* had been forced to return because of defects. The submarine arrived in the assigned patrol area on the evening of 19 June. Sea conditions were rough, and there was a temperature of 45°C and 100% humidity. Almost immediately Pelosi received a signal directing the submarine to a new area off the Somali coast. It was an unpromising assignment and Pelosi asked for confirmation, which was duly received.

No sooner had the *Torricelli* reached this new area on the 21st than she was detected and attacked with gunfire and depth charges by three British destroyers. It is possible that the British were alerted solely by the radio traffic between the submarine and Massawa, but there is also the possibility that their presence was

Capitano di Corvetta Salvatore Pelosi, the Commanding Officer of the submarine Torricelli. *(Ufficio Storico della Marina Militaire, Rome)*

due to information gathered onboard the captured *Galileo Galilei* – as was the case with the loss of the *Luigi Galvani*.

The British ships soon lost contact with the *Torricelli* but their attacks had left the Italian submarine in no condition to continue the patrol. Added to this, defects in the air-conditioning system were making the crew ill. The submarine had passed the Straits of Perim on the surface in the early hours of the 23rd when she was sighted by the sloop HMS *Shoreham*, where morale was sky-high after the part they had played in the capture of the *Galileo Galilei*. The submarine dived and escaped further damage. An hour later in the pre-dawn, helped by a full moon, Pelosi was able to see the *Shoreham* going away in the direction of Perim Island. Leaking oil from one of the submarine's tanks, which would soon give his position away, Pelosi decided that, given the general condition of his boat, his only option was to surface and go at full speed towards safety.

For a mere five minutes Pelosi was able to hope that he might be successful, but then he saw the *Shoreham* turn round and head towards him again. The sloop was almost immediately joined by a second, HMIS *Indus*, followed by three destroyers, the *Khartoum*, the *Kandahar* and the *Kingston*. Unable to dive, the submarine could either surrender or fight it out on the surface. Pelosi chose the latter. It was an unequal contest; the Italian had but one 100mm (3.9 inch) gun against the six 4.7 inch guns fitted in each destroyer and the guns in the two sloops. The submarine was the first to open fire and her second round hit the *Shoreham*, which broke off the action. The submarine fired torpedoes, but these were easily evaded. British gunnery was not good and it was nearly half an hour before they gained a hit, the shell wounding the commanding officer and putting the steering gear out of action.

At this stage Pelosi ordered his crew on deck and the submarine to be scuttled. Pelosi himself had to be helped into the sea on account of his wound, but had the satisfaction of seeing his submarine sink with its ensign still proudly flying. The crew were all rescued by two of the destroyers and taken to Aden.[10] *Capitano di Corvetta* Salvatore Pelosi was subsequently awarded the *Medaglio d'Oro al Valore Militare* for this action.

Five hours later the air vessel of the starboard wing torpedo on the after mounting on the *Khartoum* exploded. The explosion jammed the after body of the torpedo in the rear of the tube, burst the tube open and sent the forward half of the torpedo through the galley and after superstructure, where it came to rest against the winch of the minesweeping gear. The warhead did not explode but a fierce fire broke out which, fed by oil from a fractured pipe in the galley, was soon out of control. Due to the intense heat it was not possible to flood the after magazine which exploded, wrecking the stern of the ship. Attempts to beach the ship in Perim harbour failed when all power was lost and the ship settled down on an even keel with her forward guns and bridge awash.

The loss of this destroyer is often attributed to the action with the *Torrecelli*. The official enquiry stated that the torpedo air vessel exploded due to external pitting creating weaknesses in the body, caused by the effect of salt water during long periods at sea in bad weather when the torpedoes could not be pulled back and cleaned. The *Khartoum* and her sister destroyers had only recently arrived in the East Indies after arduous service in the early days of the war in the Atlantic and the North Sea.[11]

The series of disasters was not yet over for the Italians. The small submarine *Perla* (*Tenente di Vascello* Mario Pouchain) left Massawa on 19 June to patrol off Berbera and Djibouti. On the evening of the 26th she was attacked with guns and depth charges by the *Kingston*, but was not seriously damaged.[12] After the destroyer had left the scene the submarine managed to surface and then ran aground. Two days later she was attacked by the guns of the cruiser *Leander* and bombed by the ship's Walrus amphibian – surely one of the few occasions that one of these slow and ungainly aircraft ever made an operational attack. The British considered that the submarine would be out of action for months, if not a total loss. They were all the more surprised when a captured Italian Air Force officer told them that she had been refloated and towed back to Massawa for repairs.

It was an unfortunate introduction to war for the Italian submarine flotilla; in

Capitano di Corvetta Salvatori, commanding officer of the submarine Archimede *being greeted by Admiral Pavona on arrival at Bordeaux. (Ufficio Storico della Marina Militaire, Rome)*

the space of sixteen days, four of the eight boats had been sunk or captured while a fifth had been badly damaged and required extensive repairs. On the credit side, all that could be claimed was the sinking of the *James Stove* by the *Galileo Galilei*, and the attack on the *Pathan* by the *Luigi Galvani*.

Over the next eight months, until the end of February 1941, the remaining three large submarines made twenty-one unsuccessful patrols. Torpedoes were fired in only two of them; in August 1940, when the *Ferraris* fired unsuccessfully at a convoy on its way to Egypt – the resulting explosions being those of the torpedoes sinking at the end of their run rather than an indication of success – and in the attack when the *Guglielmotti* sank the *Atlas*.[13] The failure of the Italian submarines is highlighted by the number of convoys passing up and down the Red Sea in safety; in August there were four convoys in each direction, in September five, in October seven – a total of eighty-six ships northbound and seventy-two southbound.

The unfortunate *Perla* never sailed at all. Towed back to Massawa in July 1940 she was under repair until the end of the year. Extensive work was required to fit her out for sea, including repairs to the main motors which had become damaged by sea water. She had completed her sea trials when she was damaged again during an air raid on Massawa harbour on 6 January 1941. It is to the credit of the repair staff in Massawa that they were able to complete these repairs at all, let alone in the few months available to them.

By the beginning of 1941 it had become clear to the Italian Naval Command in East Africa (*MARISUPAO*) that British troops would soon be able to capture the whole of Eritrea including the two ports of Massawa and Asab. For this reason they had to make a decision about the fate of the remaining ships and submarines. The destroyers and other craft, because of their short range, had no hope of reaching a friendly port and were ordered to prepare to scuttle themselves. The initial plan was for the three surviving ocean going submarines to proceed to Japan where they would be interned, while the *Perla* was to sail for Bushire in Iran where she too would be interned. This was later changed to Diego Suarez, where it was thought that the pro-Axis Vichy authorities in Madagascar could be persuaded to provide a friendly haven.

Supermarina, the Italian Admiralty in Rome, contacted the German Naval High Command and it was agreed with Admiral Dönitz that the four submarines could use a German supply ship in the South Atlantic. The *Perla* would additionally have another rendezvous in the Indian Ocean south of Madagascar. This would enable them to reach Bordeaux in France from where they could either continue operations in the Atlantic under German control or return to Italy. It was an optimistic plan considering the poor material state of the submarines and the immense distance to be travelled, some 13,000 miles. All unnecessary equipment was removed, including the reload torpedoes, so that as much space as possible was available for sixty days' stores to be carried. Consequently the submarines were ordered to avoid all offensive action while on passage. Finally, they were given instructions that should they miss any of the rendezvous positions with the German tankers they were to proceed to the nearest neutral port to be interned.

The *Perla*, now commanded by *Tenente di Vascello* Bruno Napp, was the first to leave on 1 March, followed by the *Archimede* (*Capitano di Corvetta* Salvatori) and the *Ferraris* (*Capitano di Corvetta* Piomarta) on the 3rd, and the *Guglielmotti* (*Capitano di Fregata* Spagone) on the 4th. They travelled submerged until they were south of the Bab-el-Mandeb at the entrance to the Red Sea. Only the *Perla* was sighted and bombed by a Blenheim aircraft soon after leaving, but this did no damage. Francois di Sotto, who had only just joined the boat as a seaman, recalls that the crew were more frightened than hurt.[14]

The three larger submarines all passed through the Mozambique Channel, despite the order to refrain from offensive action and the need to be routed as far as possible from the main shipping lanes since this represented a saving of several hundred miles and a corresponding amount of fuel. In the Mozambique Channel they met with some of the worst weather of the whole trip, heavy seas causing all three submarines to heave to for some time. From there they proceeded well to the south of the African coast to a position 25° 00' South 20° 00' West – in an area

The Guglielmotti *arrives in Bordeaux from East Africa in early May 1941. The submarine returned to the Mediterranean in September of that year and was subsequently torpedoed and sunk off Taranto by HMS* Unbeaten *in March 1942. (Ufficio Storico della Marina Militaire, Rome)*

codenamed 'Andalusien' - where they were to rendezvous with the German tanker *Nordmark*.

The position was 6,600 miles from Massawa with about the same distance ahead of them before the submarines reached Bordeaux. *Kapitän zur See* Gran of the *Nordmark* found them waiting impatiently for him, sending out homing signals every four hours. His own signals telling them to cease transmitting were either not received or ignored. What made the position more dangerous was the fact that the *Nordmark*, disguised as the American tanker *Prairie*, had been overflown by a seaplane which dropped a note warning the tanker that she might be heading into danger. The aircraft, obviously from a British warship which was too close for comfort, flew off to the north west, so once Gran had collected his charges he took them off in the opposite direction.

While topping up with fuel, oil, water and extra provisions, the *Nordmark* acted as a hotel, enabling many of the Italian crews to stretch their legs, bathe and have a meal in comfort. The three submarines then went on their way, leaving the Germans to wait for the *Perla*. The final part of their route took them to the west of the Canary Islands and the Azores before turning east to Bordeaux. Although they had travelled independently they arrived almost together between 7 and 9 May after sixty-five days at sea.

The *Perla* took a route to the east of Madagascar to a rendezvous with the German raider *Atlantis* 470 miles SSE of the island on 29 March. They met up, after some difficulties, 120 miles from the original position due to a mistake by the Italian staff. The raider's captain, *Kapitän zur See* Bernhard Rogge, records[15] that the Italian crew were in low spirits and that the submarine was in a pitiable condition. He transferred food and some 70 tons of fuel, while his own crew tried to help the submariners repair some of the *Perla*'s many defects. There must have been a misunderstanding between Rogge and Napp, since the German's account states that he persuaded the latter to operate in company until 8 April, hoping that the appearance of a submarine off Durban would make a big impression on the Allies. Whatever was agreed, Napp took his submarine straight on to the next rendezvous with the *Nordmark* in 'Andalusien'.

Like the three other submarines, the *Perla* subsequently met up with the *Nordmark* and received a further ration of stores and fuel before going on to Bordeaux – of necessity she took the slightly shorter route to the east of the Azores

The crew of the Archimede *are inspected by Admiral Parona after their arrival in Bordeaux from East Africa. (Ufficio Storico della Marina Militare, Rome)*

into the Bay of Biscay. With safety not far away, it was a dangerous time for the Italians; the Bay of Biscay was heavily patrolled by the British. However, the Italians knew that their long voyage was almost over and as a result there was a natural temptation to relax their vigilance. Di Sotto recalls that they were buzzed by a German aircraft, though whether this was a deliberate attack, albeit in error, or merely a reconnaissance to check up on the Italians is not clear. Whatever the reason, it gave them all a nasty few moments. Eventually, escorted by German minesweepers, they triumphantly entered the Gironde on 20 May after eighty-one days at sea.

It had been a gruelling passage for all four submarines. Di Sotto's memory of the voyage is one of constant boredom, relieved only by the excitement of the meetings with the German tankers.

> *Life onboard was divided between one's watch station, maintaining the machinery and meals. We spent our rest time reading, listening to the news, playing cards and sleeping, waiting for the next watch. Every day the same routine, the same tasks.*[16]

This epic voyage had a curious postscript across the world in Shanghai. Lieutenant Stephen Polkinghorn RNR was captured by the Japanese on the opening day of

Tenente di Vascello Bruno Napp, the commanding officer of the Perla, *with Admiral Parona in Bordeaux. (Ufficio Storico della Marina Militaire, Rome)*

The Perla *docks in Bordeaux after arriving from East Africa in May 1941. The* Perla *later returned to the Mediterranean and was captured in Augusta in Sicily when the port fell to the British Army in July 1943; she was commissioned temporarily as HMS P712 before being handed over to the Greek Navy and renamed again as the* Matrozos. *(Ufficio Storico della Marina Militaire, Rome)*

the war in the Far East – 8 December 1941 – when his small unarmed river gunboat was overwhelmed. Life in a Japanese prisoner of war camp was never easy, but Polkinghorn recalls that he was treated marginally better than the other prisoners, possibly because word had reached his captors that his son-in-law was a famous Italian submariner, half German and half Italian, and his family included several high ranking Italian Army officers. Fritz Tamburini had met and married Stephen Polkinghorn's daughter while serving in a gunboat in China in 1937.[17] In 1941 he was the second in command of the submarine *Guglielmotti*. On arrival in Bordeaux he was sent back to Italy, where he was decorated, like so many of the crews who had made the voyage from East Africa, and given command of the *Ammiraglio Millo*. He was killed with all his crew when the submarine was torpedoed and sunk in the Mediterranean.

The arrival of the four submarines in Bordeaux brought the Italian Navy's part in the East African campaign to an end. Neither the submarines nor the surface ships had achieved significant success, as British convoys made constant use of the Red

Sea routes to Egypt. What marks the whole era as outstanding is the fact that the submarines were able to return to their home bases despite their poor mechanical condition and the debilitating effect on the crews of the previous eight months spent either at Massawa or trying to conduct useful patrols at sea against the Allies.

Little would any Italian submariner have thought that he would be back in the Indian Ocean before the war was over.

Notes:

1 Letter from the Naval Historical Branch, Ministry of Defence (NHB) to author.

2 *Axis Submarine Successes* by Jurgen Rohwer, US Naval Institute 1983.

3 NHB to author.

4 *ibid*.

5 *Attivita' dei Sommergibili Italiani in Mar Rosso* prepared by the Ufficio Storico, Rome.

6 This account is taken from the diary of an Italian Officer and found later at the scene of the accident. It was published during the war by the Admiralty in *Weekly Intelligence Reports*.

7 Commander in Chief East Indies War Diary, June 1940. (Held in the Public Record Office under reference ADM 199/383).

8 Admiralty Monthly Anti Submarine Reports, July/August 1940. (ADM199/2057).

9 *ibid*.

10 *La Marina Italiana nella Seconda Guerra Mondiale*, Volume X – The Italian Official History.

11 Report by Commander D.T. Dowler RN on the loss of HMS *Khartoum*, and the Report of the Board of Inquiry. (ADM 1/11210).

12 C-in-C East Indies War Diary June 1940. (ADM 199/383).

13 *Attivata' dei Sommergibili Italiani*.

14 Letter from Signor Francois di Sotto to author.

15 *Under Ten Flags* by B. Rogge.

16 Signor di Sotto to author.

17 Letter from Dottore A. Rostelli to author.

Three
The French and Madagascar

The French Navy took great pride in their tradition as European submarine pioneers and in the years between the two world wars they invested heavily in new construction. When war broke out again in September 1939 the French Navy had seventy-seven submarines; of these, the large ocean going boats of the *Redoubtable* class, the medium (600 tons) boats of the *Diane* class, six minelayers and the monstrous 3,000 tons *Surcouf* were the most important. About twenty of the large and medium boats, first completed in the 1920s, had been modernised in the years preceding the outbreak of war. Nevertheless, in September 1939 only forty-one submarines could be classed as first rate, including twenty-nine of the ocean boats (1,500 tons).

The French submarines suffered from the technical problem of unreliable torpedo gyros, which limited the track angle at which the torpedoes could be fired. To compensate for this tactical liability many of the boats were fitted with an external traversing mounting of up to four torpedo tubes. Another oddity was that individual classes of submarines were fitted with torpedo tubes of different sizes – 55cm (21.65 inch) and 40cm (15.75 inch) on the newer boats, while the older submarines had 45cm (17.7 inch) – with obvious logistical headaches.

Morale among the French submariners was high and much was expected from the force. Surprisingly, however, there was no centralised single submarine commander; instead the boats were allocated to the various bases on the French Atlantic and Mediterranean coasts and to Dakar in West Africa, coming under the operational command of the appropriate fleet commanders.

At the end of 1938 the submarines the *Le Phénix* and *L'Espoir* were sent on a temporary detachment from the 5th Submarine Squadron at Toulon to Saigon, proceeding via the Suez Canal. It was not intended that they should remain in the Far East for long, since the lack of air conditioning made life extremely unpleasant onboard this class of submarine in the tropics.

Within the space of a few weeks in May and June 1939 the USS *Squalus*, HMS *Thetis* and the *Le Phénix* were lost in successive major submarine accidents around the world. In the case of the *Le Phénix* there were no survivors to relate what had happened, nor was it possible to salvage the wreck. A Board of Enquiry concluded that there had been a battery explosion on diving, or shortly after. However, because of the likelihood of the outbreak of war the findings of the Board were not made public, since the French Navy did not wish to publicise possible defects in their submarines. Instead they allowed the story to circulate that the *Le Phénix* had dived with a hatch open, a version of events given more credibility by the fact that it was commonplace, when in the tropics, for a hatch to be left open when the submarine was on the surface to allow fresh air into the otherwise stifling conditions onboard the vessel.[1]

The *L'Espoir* remained on station conducting surveillance patrols off the coast of Indo-China after the outbreak of war. She was subsequently recalled to France, leaving Saigon on 2 November 1939 and calling at Djibouti before returning to Toulon via the Suez Canal.

Since Italy did not enter the war until shortly before the French surrender at the end of June 1940 and the German Navy and merchant fleet offered few targets for them, the French submarines spent many frustrating days seeking possible blockade runners. Apart from this, the force was largely wasted in non-productive operations such as escorting convoys. One submarine was lost: the *Doris* was torpedoed by the *U-9*[2] while on patrol off the Dutch coast. The German boat was commanded by *Oberleutnant* Wolfgang Lüth, a future 'ace' who would go on to play a prominent role when the U-boats reached the Indian Ocean.[3]

Under the terms of the Armistice Agreement with Germany and Italy all of the Atlantic and Channel coast of France was occupied by German forces, with the loss to the French Navy of most of their main bases and many supporting facilities in mainland France. Article Eight of the Agreement, which covered the French Navy, initially required all ships to return to their base port and be decommissioned. Over the months, intense negotiation, particularly after the British action at Mers-el-Kebir, diluted this requirement and the Navy was allowed to keep a specified number of ships and submarines in commission, mainly for policing the colonies of the French Empire. Any ships additional to these numbers were to be laid-up. Whenever French forces had to be sent abroad, either as reinforcements or to replace units that had been away for long periods, the approval of the relevant German or Italian Armistice Commissions had to be obtained, the Italians co-ordinating movements in the Mediterranean and the Red

Sea and the Germans in the rest of the world.

Any story of the French Navy during the Second World War inevitably involves the tragedy of the French defeat at the hands of the Germans in June 1940 and the bitter politics of the day which divided Frenchman from Frenchman. On one side was Marshal Pétain and his Government of France based in Vichy, while in London General de Gaulle regarded himself as the leader of the Free French, the Fighting French. All Frenchmen were haunted by the action between the British and French navies at Mers-el-Kebir in July 1940 which resulted in over 1,600 casualties, killed and wounded, on the French ships following a bombardment by the British in an attempt to ensure that the Germans did not take over any of the French fleet. The rights and wrongs of this action do not directly concern us here, though the subsequent operations do, but it is worth reminding ourselves of the mistrust and bitterness which the French felt towards the British.

France may have been defeated in June 1940 and forced out of the war but she still had an Empire to administer. Some of the French colonies declared for General de Gaulle while the remainder gave their loyalty to what they maintained was the only true authority – in Vichy. Around the Indian Ocean the French Governors in Madagascar and French Somaliland were totally committed to Vichy. The latter even went as far as to decree the death penalty for anyone rash enough to declare for the Free French, so it was hardly surprising that when *Général* Legentilhomme – a firm supporter of de Gaulle – crossed the border into British Somaliland on 2 August he had with him only a handful of men. The rather more distant colony of Indo-China initially appeared likely to join de Gaulle, but *Général* Catroux was replaced as Governor-General by *Amiral* Decroux, who remained staunchly loyal to Petain's Government in Vichy, and the opportunity was lost. The Admiral, a former submariner himself, had been the Commander in Chief of the *Forces Navales d'Extreme-Orient*.

Madagascar was by far the most important French colony in the Indian Ocean area and was destined to play a vital role in the course of the war. The island is about a thousand miles long and lies in a roughly north-south direction. At the northern end was the naval base of Diego Suarez, one of only three ports on the island. The great harbour was reputed to be large enough to act as an anchorage for the battle fleets of all the world's navies. However, it had the disadvantage of being virtually cut off from the rest of Madagascar. The other main ports were Tamatave on the east coast and Majunga on the west.

Mention has already been made of the visit to Diego Suarez of HMS *Olympus* in December 1939.[4] In June 1940 there were no French submarines in the Indian Ocean and to remedy this situation the French Admiralty persuaded the Armistice Commissions that fresh dispositions should be made. As a result the submarines *L'Espoir* and *Le Vengeur* left Toulon on 11 October 1940 and met up with the *Monge* and the *Pégase* from Bizerta before passing through the Straits of Gibraltar and heading for Dakar. They remained at Dakar until 17 December when the four submarines, in company with the tanker *Lot*, set sail for the long passage round the Cape of Good Hope to Madagascar. Like the Italian submarines which made the journey from East Africa back to Europe in early 1941[5], the submarines had no friendly ports en route where they could call and had only the tanker on which to rely for refuelling. The small convoy arrived at Tamatave on 15 January without having encountered any trouble or interference and from there went on to Diego Suarez. After a few days' rest the *Monge* and the *Pégase* proceeded across the Indian Ocean to Indo-China, accompanied by the tanker.

The Allies accorded the Vichy authorities in French Somaliland more importance than the size of the small colony would seem to warrant. Admittedly the ability to make use of the railway line which ran from Djibouti to the Ethiopian capital Addis Ababa would have helped with the problems of logistics during the British campaign to capture Italian East Africa, but although the French were close to the vital sea route up the Red Sea they represented no real threat. Nevertheless, Churchill ordered that the two ports of Obock and Djibouti be blockaded. In Cairo, General Wavell – who was responsible for any operations in the area – demurred, partly on humane grounds and partly because there were not the resources to maintain an effective blockade, but he was overruled. Until December 1941, when Japan entered the war, a nominal blockade was maintained but supplies were regularly smuggled into the colony, using Arab dhows to make trips across the Red Sea from Saudi Arabia or the Yemen. In addition many tons of food reached the colony clandestinely from Madagascar.

One of the first naval ships to arrive at Djibouti with supplies was the submarine *Le Vengeur* from Diego Suarez on 30 July 1941. On the previous day she had surprised the Free French sloop *Savorgnan de Brazza* in the act of capturing a dhow off the port of Obock. The submarine fired two torpedoes at the sloop, both of which missed. However, the incident was enough to persuade the sloop to cut the tow of her prize and she left the area without further action.

It might be said that *Lieutenant de Vaisseau* Digard, the Commanding Officer of the *Le Vengeur*, deliberately missed what was virtually a sitting target as he did not want to risk killing fellow Frenchmen. This is not very probable; there was little love lost between the two opposing groups of Frenchmen. It is more likely that the torpedoes did not run true or that there was an error in Digard's firing solution. In either case the crew of the sloop may have thought themselves lucky, while the submariners may have felt that they themselves were fortunate not to have been counter-attacked. Regardless of the outcome of this encounter it served as a timely reminder to the British that potentially hostile submarines were again present in this area.

Merchant shipping continued to pass backwards and forwards between Indo-

The French naval tanker Lot *with three of the four submarines which were to accompany her to Madagascar and Indo-China in December 1940. Note the tropical helmets worn by the crew working on deck. (Admiral Francois)*

The officers of the Le Vengeur *on the bridge. Capitaine de Corvette Digard, the commanding officer, is in the centre. (Contrôleur Général des Armées P-Y Digard)*

Two views of the 100mm gun. In calm weather, and when ploughing into a head sea. (P-Y Digard)

The gun's crew of Le Vengeur. *Note the tropical helmets tied with the name ribbon of the submarine. (P-Y Digard)*

Onboard the Le Vengeur *in the Indian Ocean, checking for damage after a storm. One of the sailors is wearing his tropical helmet while the others have the traditional French sailors' hat complete with red pompom. (P-Y Digard)*

Four submarines secured at their berth in Diego Suarez at the end of their passage from Dakar. The tanker Lot *is anchored out in the bay. The wide expanse of the anchorage and the tropical vegetation surrounding the base can be clearly seen. (Admiral Francois)*

China and France and it became obvious to the British authorities that the cargoes represented a serious leak in their blockade of German occupied continental Europe. Consequently the Royal Navy was instructed to intercept and escort French ships into port for examination. As early as January 1941 the *Sontay* was escorted into Durban, where a cargo of rubber and other contraband was seized. Another ship, the *Jean L.D.*, was similarly dealt with in Capetown.

Both the *Le Vengeur* and the *L'Espoir* carried out patrols to provide distant escort for some of the merchantmen while in the vicinity of Madagascar. Two such ships were the *Ville du Havre* and the *Ville de Tamatave* which were able to complete their voyages successfully. Less fortunate was the *Charles L.D.*, which was intercepted by the British cruiser HMS *Leander* and sent into Port Louis in Mauritius in April 1941. The *L'Espoir* was sent to patrol off the British port in the hope that the merchant ship could be recaptured, but nothing was seen of her and the submarine returned to Diego Suarez on 6 May.

As a result of these incidents the Vichy Government decided to send ships in convoy. The first of these, consisting of five merchant ships and a tanker escorted by a sloop, left Tamatave in August 1941. British intelligence thought that the escort might also include a submarine, but this was not the case. A plan to

Onboard Le Vengeur *en route to Djibouti. Some of the veteran crew are ready to take part in the 'Crossing the Line' ceremony. (P-Y Digard)*

Le Vengeur *lying alongside the* Eloran *in Djibouti in December 1941. Camouflage awnings have been draped over the submarine to provide some shelter from the sun and protection in the event of a British reconnaissance flight. (P-Y Digard)*

intercept the ships as they passed some 400 miles off the South African coast failed because of bad weather and muddled arrangements.

In late October 1941 a second convoy of six Vichy French merchant ships from Indo-China left Tamatave for West Africa and France, escorted by the sloop *D'Iberville*. On 1 November the cruisers HMS *Devonshire* and *Colombo*, together with the armed merchant cruisers *Carnarvon Castle* and *Carthage*, were ordered to carry out Operation BELLRINGER, with the task of intercepting the convoy. The next day the convoy was still in the Indian Ocean, 500 miles from the South African coast between Durban and Port Elizabeth. When intercepted by the British ships on 3 November the convoy commander in the sloop was ordered to instruct his charges to proceed to Port Elizabeth. The Frenchman refused, adding that the ships carried no contraband, only food for the French people. Reluctantly, the senior officer of the British force, in the *Devonshire*, was therefore constrained to give the French captain an ultimatum: either he ordered the convoy to heave to or the *Devonshire* would have to open fire. Wisely, the French captain bowed to superior force and ordered the convoy to stop.

The captured French ships were the merchantmen *Bangkok*, *Compiègne*, *Cap Padaran*, *Cap Vanella*, *Cap Tourque* and *Commandant Dorise*. Two South African trawlers carried out an anti-submarine patrol around the ships while the boarding parties were ferried across before taking over their charges. Some of the French Masters attempted to scuttle their ships, but the vessels were boarded and saved

The sloop D'Iberville *with the submarines* Le Vengeur *and* Glorieux *at Djibouti. (P-Y Digard)*

in time. There was no violence, only passive resistance and the boarding parties had to assume total responsibility for sailing the ships to South Africa. The *Cap Padaran*'s engines were sabotaged and the *Carthage* had to tow her into Port Elizabeth. The *Commandant Dorise*'s steering gear had been blown up, but the boarding party managed to rig hand steering and she too was taken into harbour.

The *Compiègne* was found to be loaded with 260 tons of leather, 65 tons of wax, 420 tons of graphite, 400 tons of rice, 145 tons of bark extract, 110 tons of ricin oil grain and 75 tons of mica, all of which would have been discharged at Marseilles. Who knows how much of this was intended to alleviate the hardships being suffered by the French or how much would, in fact, have been transported to Germany? In addition there were 300 tons of coffee, 797 tons of tin and 530 tons of food, as well as some general cargo, consigned to Dakar.

The British had orders to avoid any conflict with the escort if this was at all possible and the sloop *D'Iberville* was allowed to return to Madagascar.[6]

The capture of the merchantmen spelt the end of Operation BELLRINGER. Reaction in France was swift and predictably angry. The Vichy Government immediately lodged a formal diplomatic protest against the 'arbitrary and unjustified' seizure of the ships, threatening reprisals. The diplomatic protest may have been mere words but the threat of reprisals was certainly not an empty gesture and it was not long before the threat became a reality.

More submarines had already been ordered to the area. In June 1941 it had been decided to send the *Héros* (*Capitaine de Corvette* Lemaire) and the *Glorieux* (*Capitaine de Corvette* Bazoche) to Madagascar from France. At the time of BELLRINGER these two boats were already on passage to Diego Suarez. On 3 November the French Admiralty signalled that they were to patrol off the South African coast with instructions to 'attack all British warships and all British merchant ships met'.

Detailed instructions from the French Admiralty were signalled to both submarines by the Admiral in Dakar and consequently the *Glorieux* took up a position about a hundred miles to the south of Capetown.[7] Shortly after midday on 15 June Bazoche fired two torpedoes at a merchant ship, both of which missed, and the merchant ship sailed on without reporting the attack. No more ships came into range of the *Glorieux* before a shortage of fuel forced Bazoche to continue his passage to Diego Suarez.

Lemaire in *Héros* had more luck. The early morning of the 17th found the submarine on the surface 60 miles to the east of the South African port of East London. Before dawn, in a force 4 wind and an ugly sea, the navigation lights of a ship were seen approaching the submarine's position. Lemaire established that he was in contact with a merchant ship, but was unable to determine its name or its nationality. He did not wish to attack a neutral American ship and so stayed on the surface as long as possible, steering a parallel course to the merchantman. Eventually, satisfied that his target was a legitimate one, Lemaire dived and fired a single torpedo at a little over 500 yards range, aiming at the bridge. Within the submarine there was surprise at the feeble sound of the explosion and at first it was thought that the torpedo had missed. However, the unknown ship had been struck forward; the bridge crumpled and she began to sink.

Shortly after the attack Lemaire heard a radio station trying to contact a ship with the call sign 'IBVC'. As no ship was heard to answer the call Lemaire wondered if 'IBVC' could have been his target, which he had estimated to be roughly 4,500 tons. In fact the call sign belonged to the *Cape Olmo*, which was miles away and unharmed, while the ship sunk by the *Héros* was the Norwegian tanker *Thode Fagelund* of some 5,700 tons.

That same night another target was detected by the *Héros'* lookouts. Before Lemaire could make an attack the unknown ship dowsed its lights and contact was lost. Lemaire was unwilling to try and track it during the night as he believed he would be going into an area where the *Glorieux* might be operating, with the obvious risk of being attacked as a result of misidentification. He remained in the area for another two days without sighting any further targets before he too resumed his passage to Diego Suarez.[8]

In late March the Admiralty in London received reports of five more French

The L'Espoir *about to leave Diego Suarez before returning to France in early 1942. Note the tricolour painted on the side of the large conning tower for identification purposes. (Admiral Francois)*

merchant ships sailing south with their escort from the French base at Dakar and another interception was planned off the Cape, as Churchill feared that the garrison in Madagascar might be reinforced before the planned British capture of Diego Suarez could be effected. In the event it proved to be a false alarm as the convoy was destined for the Ivory Coast.

On 25 October the *Monge*, which had been sent back from Indo-China to strengthen the naval forces in Madagascar, arrived in Djibouti with more supplies and sailed again for Diego Suarez on 15 November. On the same day the *Héros* set off for Djibouti. The sloop *D'Iberville* was able to carry another 300 tons of food for the beleaguered colony and she sailed with the *Glorieux*, meeting the *Héros* which was waiting to escort them into the harbour. The *Le Vengeur* made a final trip in early January 1942 before returning to France in company with the *L'Espoir*. In February the *Héros* sailed again for Djibouti together with the *Bougainville*, formerly a German merchant ship, which carried 1,100 tons of food and live cattle. The passage was without incident as the Royal Navy was facing more pressing problems at that time following the fall of Singapore and the Japanese attack on the Dutch East Indies, and therefore made no attempt to enforce the blockade. The *Bévéziers*, which had recently arrived from Dakar,[9] made the final supply run to Djibouti by a submarine, arriving back in the first days of May, just before the British attack.[10]

Relations between the French Admiralty and the Armistice Commissions, the Italians in particular, were never cordial and usually every possible difficulty was put in the way of the French. In this vein, the deployment of another submarine to Madagascar, the *Sidi-Ferruch*, was vetoed on the grounds that the submarine being relieved had not then reached its assigned base in Toulon – indeed it was still in Madagascar! On 12 March 1942 Admiral Raeder reported to Hitler:[11]

> *The Japanese have recognised the great strategic importance of Madagascar for naval warfare…they are planning to establish bases on Madagascar in addition to Ceylon, in order to cripple sea traffic in the Indian Ocean and the Arabian Sea.*

Hitler did not think that Vichy would consent to a Japanese occupation of Madagascar but Vichy could no more prevent the Japanese from landing there than it could in Indo-China. Who knows what Marshal Pétain or Admiral Darlan, the Commander-in-Chief of the French Navy would have done had the Japanese decided to press the point? On the British side, Churchill was well aware of the dangers to the Allies' supply lines across the Indian Ocean should the Japanese try to occupy Madagascar or merely coerce the French into allowing them to use the facilities of the naval base.

In November 1940 the War Cabinet in London had discussed the possibility of gaining control of the island, which stretched across the vital shipping routes into the Indian Ocean. It was decided that, with all the other theatres of war demanding troops, there could be no question of a military expedition. Indeed, after the fiasco of the attempted joint Anglo-Free French landings at Dakar in September there was no room for any further failure. A year later, following Japanese entry into the war, Churchill recognised the island's importance as a possible Japanese objective and he was worried that the Vichy authorities on the island might easily accede to Japanese demands, as they had in Indo-China. The planning for an operation – codenamed IRONCLAD – to seize the main base at Diego Suarez began in December 1941, but it was only after many delays and cancellations that the troops set sail from the Clyde in March 1942.

Shortly before dawn on 4 May 1942 British troops began landing in Courrier Bay on the west coast of Madagascar and pushed inland, against stubborn resistance, towards their objectives around the naval base.

Although four submarines were based at Diego Suarez only one, the *Bévéziers*, was alongside in the harbour at the time of the attack, and she was sunk by the Fleet Air Arm before having a chance to get away from the jetty. All but eight of the crew of the *Bévéziers*, however, survived and joined the 4,000 army personnel in defending the base, only surrendering during the night of 6/7 May after the submarine's commanding officer, *Lieutenant de Vaisseau* Richard, had been seriously wounded by a hand grenade. The submarine herself was salvaged in 1943 but was not repaired.

Of the other three submarines, *Héros*, *Monge* and *Glorieux*, two were at sea and one was at Majunga, 350 miles to the south on the west coast. *Captaine de Vaisseau* Maerten, commanding the naval establishment at Diego Suarez, immediately recalled them, at the same time ordering them to 'torpedo any enemy ships encountered en route'. The *Héros*, 500 miles to the north and escorting a merchant ship to Djibouti, immediately turned south and made her best speed on the surface at 17 knots. It took her almost two days to reach Courrier Bay, by which time the fighting on land was nearing its end. She was then spotted by a Swordfish aircraft from the aircraft carrier *Illustrious*, depth charged and sunk. Twenty of her crew were lost, the remainder being rescued out of a shark-infested sea by HMS *Keren*, one of the assault landing ships.

The *Monge*, recalled after escorting a convoy to La Réunion, arrived off Pointe Orangea – the entrance to the harbour at Diego Suarez – at dawn on 7 May. The submarine's arrival coincided with a daring exploit by a British destroyer, HMS *Anthony*, which with considerable skill had penetrated the harbour entrance during the night and landed fifty Royal Marines on a central quay before escaping under heavy fire. This brilliant and carefully calculated dash resulted in the capture of the naval base, with its large supplies of rifles and machine guns, and the release of fifty British POWs. The main British fleet then decided to anchor

The submarine Monge. *Note the tall radio masts which are raised. (Capitaine de Vaisseau Claude Huan)*

in the harbour of Diego Suarez. En route, at eight o'clock on the morning of 8 May HMS *Indomitable* was unsuccessfully attacked by the *Monge*, which was promptly sunk by the carrier's escorting destroyers with the loss of all hands. This was especially tragic as *Captaine de Vaisseau* Maerten and the Garrison Commander, Colonel Claerebout, had by then surrendered and all fighting on land had ceased.

The fourth submarine, the *Glorieux*, made her way from Majunga and on 6 May was ordered to attack the British fleet to the west of Courrier Bay. However, the high speed manoeuvring of the British ships and their escorting destroyers kept them out of range. Two days later, and at the point of exhaustion, *Glorieux* asked Diego Suarez for instructions but naturally got no reply; then, during the night of 8/9 May, she received a signal from Vichy stating that Diego Suarez had been captured and ordering the *Glorieux* to return to Majunga and then later round the Cape to Dakar. In his report *Capitaine de Corvette* Bazoche ended by saying:[12]

All on board felt the keen disappointment I did myself at sighting the best target a submarine could ever be given without also having the chance of attacking it.

The British objective, the capture of the naval base at Diego Suarez with its magnificent harbour, had been gained. The base was virtually cut off from the rest of the island by high mountains and there was no wish to engage in the unnecessary action with the French which a further advance would entail. Altogether the French lost 3 submarines and 3 small surface warships, with 171 dead and 343 wounded.

In the event, British hopes that the French Governor-General on Madagascar would co-operate with the Allies were groundless. French casualties in the May actions had made him even more obdurate and anti-British. Nevertheless, the prime purpose of the operation – to occupy Diego Suarez and thus forestall the Japanese – had been achieved and it was decided that there was no need to initiate further operations on the island. However, Japanese submarine activity in the Mozambique Channel in the summer changed the British view and the decision was made to occupy the whole island. Fresh landings were started near Majunga in September 1942 and operations continued until November when the French finally surrendered. There were no submarine actions during this final phase for the last remaining French submarine in the Indian Ocean, the *Glorieux*, had already sailed for France.

Ironically, the Japanese did not operate again in that part of the Indian Ocean. By the end of 1942 German U-boats were able to reach the Mozambique Channel and the area retained its strategic importance.

Notes:

1 From an article by Jean Lassaque supplied to the author by *Capitaine de Vaisseau* Claude Huan.

2 The French were lucky not to have lost a second boat in an 'own goal' incident, also in the North Sea, when the *Antiope* fired three torpedoes at the *Sybylle*; one passed ahead, another stern and the third beneath the hull, clearly audible to all onboard.

3 See Chapter Eight.

4 See Chapter One.

5 See Chapter Two.

6 *War in the Southern Ocean* by L. Turner *et al*, OUP 1961.

7 Signal from *Amiraute Française* sent at 17.15 (Paris time) on 3 November 1941, copy kindly supplied by *Capitaine de Vaisseau* Claude Huan.

8 Report of *Héros'* patrol, dated 1 December 1941, forwarded to the French Admiralty by the Commander of the Submarine Group in Madagascar.

9 During the abortive Anglo-Free French attack on Dakar in September 1940 the *Bévéziers* attacked HMS *Resolution*. One torpedo of a salvo of four hit amidships while the battleship was turning under full helm, flooding a boiler room on the port side and causing a $12\frac{1}{2}°$ list. The damage necessitated the ship being sent to America for repairs and she was out of action for several months.

10 Letters to the author from *Capitaine de Vaisseau* Claude Huan and Pierre Hérvieux.

11 *Fuehrer Conferences on Naval Affairs*.

12 *The Reluctant Enemies* by Warren Tute, Collins 1990.

Four
The Dutch

For most of 1941 the Dutch Government in exile in London vainly sought a firm assurance of support from the British should the Dutch East Indies be attacked by the Japanese. All the British Government was prepared to give was a verbal statement that, in the event of a Japanese attack, help would be given 'to the best of our ability'.[1] The Americans were no more forthcoming. In these circumstances it must not be forgotten that the British were fully committed in the war against both Germany and Italy, and as a consequence there were few resources available to be sent to the Far East if the war became more widespread. Another important factor was that while the Dutch forces continued to operate under British command in Europe, in the Far East the Dutch remained under their own political and military command until the Japanese attacked.

In Singapore and Batavia (now Jakarta) the respective commanders were more pragmatic than their London-based counterparts and an Anglo-Dutch naval agreement was concluded in Singapore in April 1941, an event deprecated by the Foreign Office in London.[2] This agreement proposed that some of the Dutch submarine force based at Surabaya in Java would come under the control of the British Commander-in-Chief should the actions of the Japanese seem likely to result in a widening of the war.

Originally Dutch submarines built for home service were designated by the prefix 'O' (*Onderzeeboot*) followed by a figure in Arabic numerals, while those built for service in the East Indies had the prefix 'K' (*Kolonien*) followed by a figure in Roman numerals. The main differences in the two types were of size and range; initially, the Colonial boats were larger than those built for use in European waters to meet the requirements of operations in the East Indies. Over the years these differences were slowly eroded. As a result the five *K XIV* class submarines, built in 1932-33, had similar characteristics to the *O 16* which was built in 1935. The system changed in 1937 with the construction of the *O 19* class; these two boats, and those subsequently built, were considered suitable for employment in either European or Far Eastern waters and from then on all new construction submarines were given 'O' numbers.

The contemporary Dutch boats were slightly smaller[3] than the British 'T' class, but were of similar performance. The *O 21* class had been the first to incorporate the Dutch invention of an 'air-mast' for enabling the diesel engines to be run when the submarine was submerged; the device was later developed by the Germans as the *Schnorkel* and post-war by the British as the 'Snort'. However, in 1940 when the Dutch submarines escaped to Britain from German occupation, the British modifications included removal of the device! At that time the Dutch submarine fleet consisted of twenty-seven boats either in commission or being completed, with a further three not yet launched. Of these, fifteen were in Far East waters, though four of them were eighteen years old and hardly suitable for operations against a rampaging Japanese Navy. Most of the remainder escaped from Dutch ports to Britain.

The terms of the April agreement were brought into play when an attack by the Japanese appeared imminent on 1 December 1941. Vice-Admiral Conrad

The Dutch submarine K XII *lying at anchor before the war. Note the awning spread to provide some protection from the tropical sun. (Institute for Maritime History, MOD The Hague (I.M.H.))*

The Dutch submarine K XII. *(I.M.H.)*

Helfrich, the Dutch Commander-in-Chief, ordered the two submarines *O 16* and *K XVII* to Singapore, from where they were sent to patrol in the southern part of the Gulf of Siam. With the actual outbreak of war three more submarines, the *K XI*, *K XII* and *K XIII*, were sent to the same area to try to intercept the Japanese invasion force. Unfortunately, by the time they arrived on patrol the Japanese were already landing their troops on the east coast of Malaya. Later in the month the *O 19* and *O 20*, already on patrol to the south east of Singapore, were also diverted northwards to operate under British direction.

It is not part of this account of submarine operations in the Indian Ocean to follow in detail the actions of these boats in the Gulf of Siam. Although they achieved some successes they were not able to alter the course of the battles for Malaya and Singapore. Similarly, the remaining boats of the pre-war Dutch East Indies flotilla, which fought under Dutch command off Java, were unable to prevent superior Japanese forces landing and capturing all the islands of the Dutch colony. This small handful of submarines had by then sunk a greater tonnage of enemy shipping than both the British and American surface and submarine forces. The cost to the Dutch submariners was high.

Of the seven Dutch submarines sent to operate in defence of Malaya, four had been lost by Christmas 1941: the *O 16*, *O 20* and *K XVII* to the Japanese, while the *K XIII* was out of action following a battery explosion in Singapore. A Japanese destroyer picked up thirty-two of the crew of the *O 20* and on 1 February they arrived in Hong Kong, where they joined British and Canadian servicemen in a POW camp. The following night two officers, Lieutenants Hordijk and Idema, with a Canadian, three RNVR officers and a rating, managed to make a remarkable escape from the camp through a sewer, stealing a boat to reach the mainland. They trekked across China to Chungking and from there were flown across the Himalayas to India. Hordijk and Idema were subsequently sent to rejoin the Dutch submariners, who by then were based in Ceylon.

With the impending final surrender of the British forces in Singapore the surviving submarines returned to their base at Surabaya in Java. There were further losses before the end of the campaign which was to see the Japanese triumphant throughout the Dutch East Indies; the *K VII* had been bombed and sunk in harbour, the *K XVI* was torpedoed by the Japanese submarine *I-66* off Borneo, while the *K X*, *K XIII* and *K XVIII*, which were unfit for sea, were all destroyed in Surabaya to prevent their capture by the Japanese when the naval base was evacuated in March 1942.

The remaining seven boats all reached port safely. The *K XI*, *K XIV*, *K XV* and *O 19* went to Colombo, while the *K VIII*, *K IX* and *K XII* reached Fremantle.

The *K XII* (*Luitenant ter Zee 1e Kl.* H.C.J. Coumou)[4] remained in Surabaya to embark Rear Admiral Koenraad together with several key officers and men of the base staff, and then sailed for Colombo during the evening of 5 March. They left the burning and wrecked naval base at virtually the same time as the Japanese troops entered the town. For the next few days they successfully evaded Japanese ships and aircraft. Emergency dives became more frequent as Coumou vainly sought a way through the heavily patrolled Straits of first Bali, then Lombok and finally Alas, which led south through the island chain. On one occasion, while passing through the safe channel of a Dutch defensive minefield, the submarine had to dive quickly because of the close proximity of the enemy. On the 8th, while attempting to evade a destroyer, the submarine was illuminated by a searchlight as it dived and shortly afterwards two patterns of six depth charges exploded some 200 yards away. Two more destroyers were encountered and successfully evaded before the submarine escaped through the Sape Strait. By this time Coumou realised that he would not have sufficient fuel to reach Colombo and course was set for Fremantle, where the *K XII* arrived safely on 20 March.[5]

Lieutenant Commander Coumou handed over command of the *K XII* to Lieutenant Brunsting. Lieutenant Commander Coumou and his veteran crew were subsequently sent to Britain to take over a British built submarine, but the ship on which they were travelling was torpedoed in the Atlantic. All but Coumou and two ratings were lost.

The *K XI* (Lieutenant Commander A.H. Deketh) had been dogged by engine trouble during her last patrol and after hasty repairs in Surabaya she left for Colombo with the Captain and staff of the Submarine Base and some of the spare crew. When south of Java she came upon the survivors of the Australian destroyer HMAS *Yarra*, which had been sunk by aircraft while escorting a convoy of refugees to Australia. The submarine was already desperately overcrowded and short of fresh water but Deketh picked up twenty-eight exhausted men, many suffering badly from wounds, and took them safely to Colombo.

Ironically, it was the eventual fate of the *K XVIII* to be sunk by the British. During a patrol in the Macassar Strait in January 1942, under the command of Lieutenant Commander C. van Well Groeneveld, an attack was carried out on a Japanese destroyer and a patrol vessel escorting a merchant ship. The patrol vessel and the merchant ship were damaged but the submarine was promptly counter-attacked. During this depth charging one of the *K XVIII*'s stern torpedoes failed to discharge, leaving the engine running in the tube. Attempts to rectify the problem led to an inrush of 40 tons of water into the submarine's after compartments. The submarine eventually reached Surabaya, but had to be scuttled as repairs could not be completed before the base fell. Lieutenant Commander Groeneveld was to lose his life in the shambles of Surabaya dockyard just before the base fell to the advancing Japanese troops. He volunteered to investigate a report of an unexploded bomb which had fallen in the torpedo workshop. Shortly afterwards the building was wrecked by a terrific explosion. The *K XVIII* was subsequently raised by the Japanese and the hulk converted to an air warning radar picket. Towed by a trawler, the rusty old submarine was part of a small convoy sighted by HMS *Taciturn* in the Java Sea on 13 June 1945. In water which was too shallow for a submerged attack, the British boat surfaced and engaged the force, expending over two hundred rounds of 4-inch ammunition. The old *K XVIII* was one of the victims.

At Colombo the Dutch submarines again came under British command and joined the only two Royal Navy submarines in the area, the *Truant* and the *Trusty*. The old depot ship HMS *Lucia* provided accommodation for the British crews while the *Columbia* gave support to the Dutch crews and their submarines. They were joined by the *O 23*, recently arrived from England.

The pressing problem for the submarines was the detection of any Japanese threat towards Ceylon. As it transpired, the Japanese fleet which attacked Colombo and Trincomalee at Easter 1942 sailed undetected south of Java and to the west of Sumatra. In two overwhelming air attacks, which fortunately were not followed up with another invasion, the embryo submarine flotilla remained unscathed except for the *Lucia*. The depot ship was hit by a single bomb which passed through the hull without exploding but which meant that the *Lucia* had to sail to Bombay for repairs.

After the fall of France in 1940 the Ministry of Economic Warfare was charged with the task of '[taking] every possibility of attacking potential enemies by means

The Dutch submarine O 19. (I.M.H.)

other than the operation of military forces.' Winston Churchill was determined that the enemy should be given no respite wherever he might be in the vast areas of conquered territory; Europe was to be set ablaze. The Special Operations Executive (SOE) was born. With the entry of Japan into the war the SOE had to have a similar organisation in India and Ceylon, where it was eventually came to be known as Force 136.

For Force 136 there were theoretically just two ways of inserting any operational parties behind the Japanese lines: by air, or by submarine. In 1942 there were no suitable aircraft in the Far East that could carry out this mission, so they had to rely on the Navy. If any landings were to be carried out clandestinely then they had to be from a submarine, and if they were to be from a submarine then it would have to be a Dutch submarine, as prior to late 1943 these were the only ones available. By January 1943, when the first such operation took place, all the Dutch submarines which had escaped the early debacles of 1941 and 1942 had left the area for badly needed refits and repairs. They had been replaced by the *O 21, O 23* and *O 24*.

The plan for the first clandestine operation was for an intelligence party to make an appreciation of conditions in the Andaman Islands under the Japanese with the expected reconquest of the Islands to follow at a later date.[6] The operation was given the codename BALDHEAD/BUNKUM. The Andaman Islands cover an area of 2,508 square miles, stretching in a chain on a north-south axis. In addition to the 4 main islands there are about 200 small islets of varying sizes – some inhabited, some not. The whole group lies in the south east of the

Bay of Bengal, about 850 miles east of Ceylon – three and half days' steaming at 10 knots. To the south and separated from the Andamans by the Ten Degree Channel lie the Nicobar Islands. Both groups were an administrative part of India and had been evacuated by the British on 12 March 1942, just four days after the Japanese had captured Rangoon. The Japanese did not begin their occupation of the islands until the end of the month.

The submarine chosen to land the military party for this operation was the *O 24*, one of the boats that had escaped from Holland in May 1940. From June 1941 until the end of the year the submarine had operated in the Mediterranean, though before being deployed she had been refitted to fire British torpedoes. In January 1943 the Commanding Officer of the *O 24* was Lieutenant Commander W.J. de Vries, who had been awarded the DSC for his part in the sinking of the *U-95* in the Mediterranean in November 1941, when he was the First Lieutenant of the *O 21*.

The landing party for BALDHEAD/BUNKUM consisted of five British and Indian Army personnel under the command of Major Denis McCarthy, who had previously served for five years as the Commandant of the Military Police Battalion and as District Superintendent of Police in the Andaman Islands. In addition there were some two tons of stores, all of which had to be fitted into an already crowded submarine.[7]

The *O 24*, with its military party and stores embarked, sailed from Colombo on 14 January 1943. For the first two days the submarine remained on the surface making the best possible speed towards the operating area. Thereafter they travelled dived by day to avoid any risk of being sighted by a Japanese reconnaissance plane; by night it was safe to proceed on the surface. On the fourth evening the *O 24* made a landfall and de Vries was able to identify the landing beach on the west coast of Middle Andaman Island. Once darkness had fallen the submarine surfaced and the whole party was put ashore without any difficulty; by midnight they had set up their first camp near a stream in the jungle, well back from the beach. The submarine had then completed its mission and returned to Colombo on the 24th, having followed the same routine as on the outward passage.

Before returning to the Andamans to pick up Major McCarthy and his party the *O 24* carried out one operational patrol on the route of Japanese traffic between Rangoon and Singapore. A number of patrol craft were seen during the first few days and these were carefully avoided. On 21 February a northbound ship of 4,000 tons was sighted and attacked with the gun; several hits were obtained which left the steamer heading towards the shore, listing and in a sinking condition. The name of the submarine's target and its eventual fate are not known; available Japanese records make no mention of the attack and, indeed, it is not even mentioned in Alden's extensive record of Allied submarine attacks.[8]

Lieutenant de Vries is decorated by Admiral Sir Max Horton with the DSC. The award was made in recognition of his service as First Lieutenant of the O 21, which had sunk the German U-95 east of Gibraltar in November 1941. (I.M.H.)

On 21 March de Vries again cautiously approached the rendezvous which he had previously agreed with McCarthy's party ashore.

Two canvas squares had been placed prominently on the beach as a signal that all was well. When the submarine sighted them her periscope was to be raised to its full extent and then lowered. Upon seeing this the shore party would remove the canvas squares. Precisely at the prearranged time Major McCarthy was delighted to sight the submarine's periscope. Delight changed to surprise as more and more of the periscope was exposed until eventually most of the submarine's conning tower was visible as well. It was some minutes before the submarine was again fully submerged. Mystified, McCarthy and his men removed their identification marks and it was not until later when they were all onboard that they learnt that the submarine had grazed a coral reef, causing her to surface involuntarily and to tear off the asdic dome.

Onboard the submarine was a medical officer in case any of the party should be ill after their sixty-five day sojourn in the jungle with the constant threat of being attacked by the Japanese garrison. Unfortunately, at the crucial time the doctor was seriously ill with malaria. Within minutes of meeting him McCarthy found himself administering an intravenous injection! Because of fears that the location might have been compromised to the Japanese, it was decided that the campsite should be demolished and all remaining stores buried. It was an onerous task, made even worse by the fact that the extra 'spoil' from the excavations had to be carefully disguised before the work was complete. The job took a full day, with the submarine remaining dived offshore while it was finished. Once again personnel had to be ferried back to the submarine before de Vries took the O 24 to the site of another proposed base camp on South Andaman Island. A periscope reconnaissance showed that it was not in fact suitable, and an alternative was found five miles further south.

The following night nearly three tons of stores were landed and hidden at the new site. The submarine had brought a party of six soldiers onboard for this purpose, their contribution was vital as the work involved was enormous. Not only had the stores to be transferred from the submarine to the shore but they also had to be hidden from accidental discovery by the Japanese and protected from marauding natives, animals, insects and the elements. An additional 2,500 lbs was left onboard the crowded submarine as de Vries headed back to Colombo. The operation marked the end of the first successful landing and recovery of Allied personnel in Japanese occupied territory.

The next operational party to be landed was destined for Malaya; again the party had to travel by submarine, again Dutch. The operation – known as GUSTAVUS I – involved the landing of one British officer and five Chinese together with their radio and a vast miscellany of stores, including two folboats.[9] The party was led by Captain John Davis, a former police officer in Singapore and now attached to the Indian Army. Inside the submarine considerable ingenuity was required to stow everything in places where it would not interfere with essential equipment and the loading of torpedoes nor adversely affect the trim of the submarine. It was planned that a junk should be commandeered to land the party rather than trying to rely on the risky transfer into folboats for the journey inshore. Once again the submarine chosen was the *O 24*.

The *O 24* sailed on 11 May 1943. The first eight days of the patrol passed without incident but then, in the small hours of 19 May, soon after the submarine had surfaced for the nightly battery charge, an enemy merchant ship, escorted by a patrol vessel, appeared out of one of the many rain squalls some sixty miles from Diamond Point in Sumatra. As he was unable to close the target, which was at a range of about three and a half miles, without risking being seen against an almost full moon, de Vries dived the submarine and prepared to fire a bow salvo. Five minutes later he fired but there were no explosions to indicate his success – he had underestimated the target's speed and all four torpedoes had passed astern. Both enemy ships seemed unaware of the attack so de Vries surfaced but was unable to gain a new firing position.

The *O 24* then spent three hours shadowing another Japanese patrol vessel, during which time the submarine had to manoeuvre constantly to close the enemy craft while avoiding being silhouetted against the moon. It is an indication of de Vries' skill that not only was he able to identify the enemy as an armed trawler about 120 feet in length but was later able to forward with his patrol report a precisely drawn sketch of the enemy for the use of other commanding officers liable to operate in the area.

Five days later the *O 24* was in position to land the GUSTAVUS party in Perak. It was to be another example of how the best laid plans in war can so easily come unstuck in practice. A junk was contacted and boarded as set out in the orders but the crew proved too old – or too stupid – to understand what was required and the landing had to be carried out using the folboats. A careful scrutiny by periscope showed that the beach appeared to be deserted and suitable for a landing, but in such cases there was always the fear that the landing party might be heading straight into a trap. All the stores were laboriously brought up onto the submarine's casing before being paddled ashore in the two folboats. It was an anxious time for de Vries and his crew, with the fore hatch open and all the stores on the casing; the submarine was in no state to dive quickly if the Japanese should be sighted. In any case, close inshore as they were, the water was too shallow for safe submerged operations. Fortunately for de Vries, no such emergency action was required and Captain Davis and the rest of his party were landed safely.

It was the first British landing in Malaya since the ignominious capitulation at Singapore fifteen months earlier, and had been carried out 1,500 miles from base.

The return to Ceylon was uneventful and the *O 24* was safely back in harbour by 31 May.

In mid-June the *O 23* (Lieutenant Commander A.N. Valkenburg) sailed to carry out GUSTAVUS II, a comparatively simple operation which would bring Captain Davis back to Ceylon. Before going to the rendezvous position with the shore party, Valkenburg carried out a short patrol off Arn Bay in Sumatra. The next day a defect put the port diesel engine out of action and two days later, while chasing a possible target on the surface at night, the starboard engine developed a fault which took time to remedy and enabled the target to escape.

Davis had managed to persuade a junk to take him to meet the submarine and, after the exchange of the correct recognition signals, Valkenburg took the *O 23* as close as possible to the other craft and Davis was able to board. After nearly a month in the jungle he was suffering from a painful skin irritation but was otherwise well. The transfer had been made in some haste, as what appeared to be a small convoy of Japanese ships had been sighted to the south and Valkenburg was anxious to try and make an attack. As no personnel had been landed on this trip he decided that the specified ban on attacks – twenty-four hours before and forty-eight hours afterwards – which had been ordered for these special operations need not be observed. Eventually two torpedoes[10] were fired on an ideal track angle at 700 yards range at a small tanker. It seemed impossible that both could miss. However, the camouflage adopted by the Japanese had led Valkenburg to believe that the tanker was sailing more deeply laden than was the case and both torpedoes ran under the target. There was no reaction by the enemy other than starting a furious zig-zag and the *O 23* was able to leave the area and return safely to Ceylon.

Usually it was the actual landing of a party on an enemy held coast that produced periods of the greatest anxiety and it was then that the best plans could go awry. For the men forming the GUSTAVUS III party and the crew of the submarine *O 23* the panic came before they had even left their bases in Ceylon. John Davis, by then a major, and three Chinese were to land from the submarine by transferring to a local junk, as had been the intention in the previous operation. Before leaving, the party trained at a camp near Trincomalee. This gave them ample opportunity to practise using the folboats which they planned to take with them in case it was not possible to use a junk. Their camp was 140 miles from Colombo but it was considered that the submarine would easily be able to pick them up on the way to the operational area.

Some days before the operation was due to start intelligence was received which meant that a submarine had to be on patrol off Port Blair in the Andamans by first light on 27 July 1943, and the only submarine available was the *O 23*. To meet that deadline it was essential for the submarine to sail from Colombo that day with the GUSTAVUS party already embarked. The submarine was at twelve hours notice for sea, but by a Herculean effort it was ready to proceed six hours after Valkenburg received his instructions. Instead of picking them up at Trincomalee as planned, the landing party had to be brought to Colombo and the Navy arranged for a Catalina aircraft to fly them there – it had to be an amphibian to take off from Trincomalee harbour and land on grass. The aircraft had to fly from Colombo, pick the party up and fly back again, landing at the deserted race course where there were no landing lights; the aircraft therefore had to be back before darkness fell. By chance the Air Officer Commanding had heard of the flight and had promptly cancelled it, believing that it had been sent to fly an army leave party to Colombo! The AOC then had to be tracked down – he was at lunch – before orders could be issued to reinstate the flight.

When John Davis and his men finally reached the docks to embark in the submarine they found that the signal plan had not arrived; incredibly, it had been delivered to another quay. When it eventually reached them, their radio set had to be tested and only then could the party embark. The O 23 sailed just before ten o'clock that night – several hours late.

Almost immediately the submarine ran into a storm, with heavy seas frequently pooping the boat and forcing Valkenburg to order the conning tower hatch to be shut to avoid the seas flooding the control room below. The bad weather and the fact that they could only run on the battery with the hatch shut meant that the O 23 might not be able to reach the ordered patrol position in time. When the seas moderated it was noticed that the submarine was losing fuel oil and leaving a conspicuous oil slick. The fault was found in a partially fractured vent pipe, but as this was under water even with the boat running on the surface, there was no chance of repairing the trouble before returning to harbour. It was decided to transfer as much oil as possible to other tanks and then dump the remainder. The process had to be done with the submarine dived and was completed in a few hours, but by then the submarine was even further behind schedule. A leaking air valve on a torpedo, which had to be pulled back and replaced by a reload, added to their troubles.

By 4.30 on the morning of 29 July the O 23 was still fifty-five miles from Port Blair, with no hope of reaching her assigned position before dawn. It was then that Valkenburg sighted the silhouette of a ship about two miles away and decided upon a bold surface attack. The target appeared to be a large warship, with a single funnel amidships and two masts, the forward one being an easily identifiable pagoda. It was thought that the target was either the training ship *Kasii* or the minelayer *Itsukushima*. Just before the submarine reached a firing position a brilliant searchlight illuminated a path just to port of the submarine and Valkenburg dived before being detected. The attack had to be abandoned as there was no chance of using the periscope in the dark. The accuracy of the searchlight when it was first switched on suggested that the Japanese ship might have been fitted with an early type of radar.

After three more days in the area the *O 23* began a surface passage to the rendezvous for the GUSTAVUS III operation, the overcast sky reducing the likelihood of being spotted by long-range air reconnaissance. The operation was carried out on 4 August. A rendezvous was made with a junk identified by a red blanket spread over the port quarter, and John Davis was allowed to use the periscope to give a positive identification of some of the members of the reception party which were onboard. All that then remained was to follow the junk until nightfall.

The final phase of the operation proved to be the simplest part of the patrol. Davis and his Chinese assistants were transferred to the junk, which then disappeared into the night for its shore landing; the submarine turned towards Penang, where it hoped to find a worthwhile target to complete the patrol. An abortive attack was carried out, again on the surface, with Valkenburg vainly trying to close the range to his target before the enemy opened fire; five shells, in rapid succession, passed over the submarine, forcing it to dive. By this time the earlier problem of leaking oil was causing a critical fuel situation and Valkenburg headed for Colombo.

On 12 September 1943 the *O 24* left Colombo for another operation, GUSTAVUS IV, in which Captain Richard Broome would join Major Davis in Malaya. On the 20th de Vries carried out a reconnaissance of a small uninhabited island with a view to its possible use as a rendezvous position for future operations. That afternoon a junk was sighted and identified as the one which they were due to meet, and John Davis himself was recognised onboard. However, before any transfer could take place a small convoy of at least three ships and its escort was sighted to the southward. There was nothing de Vries could do as he was still forbidden to carry out an attack for a period of twenty-four hours before a special operation and for forty-eight hours afterwards. After dark Captain Broome and all his stores were safely put aboard the junk and one of the Chinese members of Davis' party was embarked to be taken back to Ceylon.

The remainder of the patrol was without success. De Vries looked for the convoy in Penang but was unable to find it – though a few days later the *Tally Ho* did, and sank one of the ships.[11] A surfaced Japanese submarine, believed to have been one of the *I-61* class, was seen passing close astern of the *O 24*, but on a dark night and with the radar out of action the target had been sighted too late and de Vries had no time to make an attack. The *O 24* was back in Colombo on 3 October.

De Vries carried out one more special operation in this series in November, going to the area between Penang and the One Fathom Bank. Again a junk was used to ferry the party of one British officer and a Chinese civilian ashore. The operation – GUSTAVUS V – was beset with problems of an unattended rendezvous, faulty equipment and Japanese patrols, but the two agents were eventually put ashore in Perak. On return to Colombo the *O 24* was considered unfit for further operations and she was sailed for a refit in the United States.

This was the last of the special operations carried out by the Dutch submarines from Ceylon. Of the other Dutch submarines which had been in Ceylon, the *O 21*, which had claimed two successes against merchant shipping in the Malacca Strait, sailed for Australia in July 1943 to work under American Commander Submarines, South West Pacific Area, for the Dutch intelligence services in the Dutch East Indies. The *O 23* returned to the United Kingdom for a refit in the November of that year.

The *K XII*, which had reached Australia after the Japanese capture of the D.E.I., was also involved in special operations.[12] However, the toils of war ensured that the *K XII* had to undergo maintenance and docking before she was fit to undertake more patrols and this was carried out first in Melbourne and then in Sydney. On 18 August 1942 Lieutenant Brunsting received orders to take a landing party from Australia to Java – Operation MACKEREL. After embarking the landing party at Cairns and fuelling at Darwin the submarine sailed for Java. The threat of detection by enemy aircraft meant that the *K XII* travelled submerged by day and surfaced by night. When they arrived off the beach which had been designated for the landing, Brunsting carried out a careful reconnaissance through the periscope to assure himself and Lieutenant van Arcken, who was to lead the party ashore, that it was safe for the landing to take place. That night Brunsting took the submarine in to within 1,000 yards of the beach before sending van Arcken and his two companions ashore.

The *K XII* then proceeded to Exmouth Bay in north-west Australia to top up with fuel and fresh water before going on to Fremantle, arriving safely on 23 September.

Another operation was carried out in mid-November, with the *K XII* sailing from Fremantle. Two landing parties – codenamed TIGER I and TIGER II – were put ashore in southern Java, each consisting of a Dutch Lieutenant and two Indonesians. This patrol meant that the submariners were at sea for a month before returning to Fremantle. A third operation – TIGER III – was carried out in February 1943, and a fourth patrol was undertaken in April and May 1943 to land two more secret parties in Java – TIGER IV and TIGER V. By this time the material state of the submarine was such that it could not be relied upon to undertake any further operations with safety. The *K XII* was therefore paid off and it was proposed that if any more special parties were to be landed in Java then a US submarine would be made available to do this.

The Dutch submarines carried out their share of operational patrols for the remainder of the war, either from Trincomalee or Fremantle. However efficiently the landing of special parties behind the lines had been carried out, there must have been considerable relief on the part of the Dutch submariners when no more such operations were ordered, although the British submarines continued to perform this task for the remainder of the war. Besides requiring the submarine's Commanding Officer to forego the chance of attacking the enemy both before and after landing any personnel on the enemy coast, there was the added risk to the submarine of operating close inshore in shallow water where there was the ever present danger of meeting enemy patrols. This was compounded by the inherent risk of any rendezvous being compromised. Flag Officer, Submarines, Rear Admiral C.B. Barry, summed up his views when commenting on the report of one such operation:

I deplore the necessity for exposing submarines to such grave risks and trust that the results achieved justify not only these risks but the time lost to offensive operations more in keeping with their true role as submarines.

Shortage of spare parts for the engines and other vital equipment forced the Dutch to decommission several of their submarines in Britain and Australia in order to cannibalise them for spares. Four British submarines were loaned to the Dutch to enable them to make use of their highly trained crews: one 'S' class, two 'T' class and a 'U' class. HMS *Talent* was one of these and became the *Zwaardvisch* commanded by Lieutenant Commander H.A. Goossens, who had earlier commanded the *O 14* in Norwegian and Arctic waters. After a short patrol off the east coast of Sumatra Goossens had taken the submarine to Fremantle.

Soon after dawn on 6 October 1944 the *Zwaardvisch* was on patrol off Surabaya when a German submarine was sighted on the surface, steering a steady course at about 14 knots. Eleven minutes after sighting the enemy Goossens fired a salvo of six torpedoes at a range of 900 yards. One hit was obtained and afterwards some survivors could be seen in the water, and twenty-seven Germans were picked up.[13] It was found that the victim was the *U-168*, under the command of *Kapitänleutnant* Helmuth Pich, bound for operations around the Australian coast. The Germans also helpfully told their rescuers that the Japanese air patrols never started before 11.00! While two fishing vessels were rounded up, the Germans were given soap to wash off the oil that had covered them during their swim, and were then given fresh clothes and drinks. Pich, his Engineer Officer, the Second Watch Officer, the doctor and an injured seaman were kept onboard the *Zwaardvisch* for the next three weeks before the submarine returned to Fremantle. They were favourably impressed with conditions onboard the Dutch boat compared with those to which they were accustomed. The remainder of the surviving German crew were sent ashore in the fishing boats.

On this patrol the *Zwaardvisch* achieved a second success when she sank the Japanese minelayer *Itsukushima*, the ship previously met by the *O 23* off the

The O 19 firmly aground on a reef while returning from patrol in 1945. The forecasing of the USS Cod, *which rescued the crew after all valuable equipment had been destroyed, can be seen in the foreground. (I.M.H.)*

Andamans at the end of July 1943. Goossens was later awarded the *Militaire Willems Orde*, the highest Dutch award for gallantry.

By the end of the war Dutch submarines were no longer attached to the submarine flotilla based in Trincomalee, while at Fremantle the *O 21* and *O 24* had joined the *Zwaardvisch*. Sadly another boat, the *O 19*, joined the long list of Dutch submarines that became casualties of the war, though in this case the boat had run aground on a reef while on passage from Fremantle to Subic Bay in July 1945. The USS *Cod* (SS-224) went to her assistance but, despite determined efforts, the Dutch boat could not be towed clear. All equipment was destroyed in order to prevent it falling into the hands of the enemy and the crew were then taken onboard the American submarine. The *O 19* had been in action from the beginning of the war against Japan and it was a great misfortune that this veteran was unable to be present at the end of hostilities.

The last patrol of the war carried out by a Dutch submarine was by the *O 21* (Lieutenant F.J. Kroesen) off the south and north-west coasts of Java between 7 July and 8 August 1945. Kroesen went to an area between the northern end of the Sunda Strait and Batavia, but his only encounter with the enemy was on the 29 July, when the submarine engaged two coasters in a gun action which had to be broken off when the gun jammed. Both ships had been hit but they managed to escape by going into water which was too shallow for the submarine. After receiving her recall the *O 21* was able to make an uneventful transit of the Sunda Strait on the surface, an indication of how far the Japanese power had waned since those heady days of March 1942 when they had captured Java and the Japanese Navy and Air Force had reigned supreme in the area. The *O 21* finally reached Fremantle on 8 August, having spent thirty-two days at sea, steaming over 6,000 miles and sinking a small coaster along the way.

Notes:

1 There are numerous papers on this subject in the PRO under many references, including CAB 66/19, PREM 3/326 and ADM 1/11326.

2 In CAB/80/28.

3 The *K XI* class had a surface displacement of 611 tons, the *K XIV* class were of 771 tons, and the *O 16* class displaced 1,170 tons. For comparison the first batch of the British 'T' class displaced 1,326 tons.

4 *Luitenant ter Zee 1e KL* equates to the British rank of Lieutenant Commander. As the Dutch submariners were operating under British or American control the anglicised form of Dutch ranks has been used.

5 *De Koninklijke Marine in de Tweede Wereld-Oorlog: De Acties der Nederlandse Onderzeeboten onder Brits en Amerikaans Operationeel Bevel.* (Netherlands Official History)

6 No such operation to recapture the Andaman Islands took place and the islands remained in Japanese occupation until the end of the war.

7 Details of these clandestine operations to land agents in the Andaman Islands and on the coast of Malaya by the Dutch submarines are taken from Ian Trenowden's *Operations Most Secret*, Crecy Books Ltd 1978.

8 *U.S. Submarine Attacks in World War 2* by John Alden, US Naval Institute Press, 1989.

9 The original folboat was a two-man collapsible canoe built pre-war for sport. It had a wooden frame and rubberised canvas cover, but was fragile, easily punctured and not very suitable for active service as there were no buoyancy aids and the cockpit was uncovered. As the war progressed the folboat was extensively modified for different operations, each having characteristics suitable for the operation for which it was required. There was even a Motor Submersible Canoe, or 'Sleeping Beauty', though it was never used successfully on an operation and was regarded as being dangerous by those who used them on trials!

10 *Operations Most Secret*.

11 See Chapter Seven.

12 Netherlands Official History.

13 *Shooting the War* by Otto Giese, Leo Cooper 1994

Five
The Japanese

At the time of the attack on Pearl Harbor the Japanese Navy had sixty operational submarines. Their early successes in the war in the Far East did not match their expectations, as was also the case with the Americans and the Dutch. However, unlike the Americans and the Dutch they failed to improve upon their record and in general did not produce the results that might have been expected of them by either their Emperor or their enemies. Most of their operations were carried out in the waters of the Pacific Ocean – although not exclusively, for the significance of the Indian Ocean was not lost on the Japanese.

Neither the characteristics of the Japanese submarines nor the expertise of the submariners can entirely explain their failure to become an important factor in the maritime war in the Far East. It is worth mentioning that, after the war was over, the Japanese officers themselves admitted that their boats were slow to dive and, once submerged, were not easily manoeuvrable. The safe diving limit was little more than 300 feet, shallower than that of the Americans but similar to the restrictions on many of the British and Dutch boats. However, they had both the speed and the range to cover the vast distances involved in oceanic patrols. The equipment fitted was basic; for instance they had no radar. On the other hand, they had fearsome torpedoes[1] that were fast, long range and reliable. All the submarines were armed with deck guns and, uniquely, many carried a small aircraft for reconnaissance.

Japanese doctrine required the submarines to operate under a more rigid control than their enemies; their orders were more tightly directed towards sinking the enemy capital ships – although, as will be seen, they had no inhibitions about attacking merchant vessels. Some Japanese submarines were designed and constructed so that a flotilla commander, who could be as senior as a Rear Admiral,[2] would be embarked to conduct the operations of several submarines in distant waters. Even in this concept the Japanese followed faulty dogma, as there was no attempt to co-ordinate attacks in the fashion of the German wolf packs; instead, they tried to control the several submarines working loosely together in a large area. Since the group commander himself was afloat in one of the submarines and therefore far removed from headquarters, his own information was necessarily limited. In addition, the system required the individual submarines to be surfaced each night to pass radio messages to and from the commander. These radio transmissions were open to interception by direction finding and their content to crypto-analysis or decryption, though there is little evidence that this was in fact the case.

The rigid tactics employed by the Japanese submarines are a prime example of an astonishing lack of flexibility in Japanese strategic and tactical planning. Even the huge harvest of destruction reaped by the German U-boats did not inspire the Imperial Japanese Navy (I.J.N.) to change their methods and attack the long American supply lines. It took a German naval officer to appreciate in full the opportunity his Japanese allies were wilfully missing, considering all that the U-boats, rarely operating in large numbers, had been able to achieve in the Atlantic from 1939-43. Vice Admiral Paul Wenneker, the Naval Attache in Tokyo, noted:

> *I suggested the desirability of attacking the route between Honolulu and the west coast [of America] because that would force the use of convoys and would force the withdrawal of many escorts from the Western Pacific.*
>
> *We arranged for one full Japanese submarine crew to be sent to Germany for training. They had, I think, very good training in German boats and in German attack methods, but unfortunately got caught in the North Atlantic while returning to Japan.*

Japanese submarines were of three different types. First there were the large ocean going boats, whose numerical names were prefixed by the letter 'I', which was the Romanisation of the first letter of the traditional Japanese syllabary and written like the Greek *lambda*. The next type were rather smaller submarines, known as the 'RO' class, the second Japanese letter. A third type, which included both coastal submarines and midgets, was known by the third Japanese letter 'HA'.

In January 1942 the submarines of the 5th Submarine Squadron of the I.J.N. were ordered to leave their base at Camranh Bay in Indo-China to conduct operations in the Indian Ocean and then proceed to a new base at the recently captured Malayan port of Penang. The *I-59*[3] and *I-60* were instructed to head straight for Penang, passing near Christmas Island and then up the west coast of Sumatra. However, on 17 January the *I-60* was detected and blown to the surface in the southern entrance to the Sunda Strait after an accurate depth charge attack by the British destroyer *Jupiter*. The submarine came up so close that at first the guns of the *Jupiter* could not be depressed far enough to bear on the target. The Japanese submarine was finally overwhelmed by the fire power of the destroyer, becoming the first Japanese warship to be sunk by a British ship. While proceeding up the coast of Sumatra the *I-59* (Lieutenant Commander T. Yoshimatsu) actually entered Sabang roads and torpedoed a ship. The *I-62* (Lieutenant Commander Takaichi Kinashi) and *I-64* (Lieutenant Commander Tsunayashi Ogawa) headed towards Ceylon and then operated off the coast of India between Madras and Cochin before reaching Penang in early February. During this period the two boats sank seven ships between them. The *I-65* (Lieutenant Commander Hakue Harada) and *I-66* (Lieutenant Commander Z. Yoshitome) went up the west coast of Sumatra and remained in the northern entrance to the Malacca Straits, as it had been erroneously reported that a British battleship was expected to sail from Singapore. The *I-65* then went directly to Penang while the *I-66* went to an area off Rangoon before returning to its new base. Japanese submarines were thus introduced to the Indian Ocean, sinking ten ships in January and five in February.

After the attack on Pearl Harbor Vice Admiral Chuichi Nagumo's Carrier Striking Force returned to Japan to prepare for the next attack, the aim of which was to eliminate any threat from the British in the Indian Ocean by finding and sinking the fleet and by striking at targets in Colombo and Trincomalee. Nevertheless the impending presence of this force became known to both British and American intelligence through the efforts of the code breakers. Additional Japanese submarines were sent to Penang to reconnoitre the area around Ceylon and up the west coast of India. The reinforcements consisted of the Second Submarine Squadron, under Rear Admiral Hisashi Ichioka, comprising five submarines: *I-2, I-3, I-4, I-6* and *I-7*. The *I-5* joined them later after completing repairs, having been bombed earlier by Japanese aircraft.[4] The *I-7* additionally carried a seaplane, and it had been intended that this would fly a reconnaissance of Colombo and Trincomalee before the strikes by the carrier aircraft. However, this had to be abandoned because of increased activity by British aircraft in anticipation of the Japanese attack and the difficulty in handling the seaplane in the rough seas.[5]

All of these submarines returned to Singapore without sighting the British fleet and having achieved only limited success. The *I-2* (Lieutenant Commander Hiroshi Inada) sank a merchant ship near the port of Padang and then another off the port of Trincomalee, where it had been assigned the task of making weather reports for the aircraft carriers. The *I-3* (Commander K. Tonozuka), in a similar role off Colombo, attacked a small convoy on 7 April but only damaged one ship in a gun action; the following day another steamer was sunk by a torpedo. The *I-7* (Commander K. Koizumi), despite being unable to fly off its aircraft, sank one merchant ship. The other three submarines patrolled off the west coast of India northwards towards Bombay and near the Maldive Islands, between them sinking seven ships. On the other hand, Admiral Nagumo's carrier strike on Ceylon at Easter was vastly more successful, causing considerable damage ashore, virtually wiping out British air power in the island and sinking a carrier and two cruisers while damaging other ships. Japanese losses in this spectacular operation amounted to a mere seventeen aircraft. Despite these successes the elderly British battleships escaped undetected, and although inferior to the Japanese ships they remained a potential threat.

Meanwhile, the original group of submarines based at Penang had also been active in the Bay of Bengal. The British, hard pressed in all theatres of war, had few anti-submarine vessels available to provide escorts for all the merchant ships using the busy ports on the coast. In the circumstances it was fortunate that losses were not heavier.

One of the victims was the *Rooseboom*, a small Dutch vessel of just over a thousand tons. The steamer had normally been engaged on the coastal run between ports in Java and Sumatra. At the end of February 1942 she was escaping to Ceylon from Batavia and had been ordered into the Sumatran port of Padang to pick up evacuees, both military and civilian, Dutch as well as British. Everyone was packed onboard like sardines, sleeping almost on top of one another on deck or crammed into the tiny cabins. No one knows the exact number of those onboard. Just after midnight on 1 March – the third evening out and only forty-eight hours from Ceylon – the *Rooseboom* was struck by a single torpedo from Lieutenant Commander Yoshimatsu's *I-59*. The lifeboats on the port side were wrecked and could not be lowered; of the two on the starboard side one crashed into the sea and was smashed, leaving just one lifeboat available for the survivors. Built to carry twenty-eight people, there were eighty onboard with a further fifty hanging on to the outside waiting for a vacancy. By the time the lifeboat had drifted a thousand miles back to the Sumatran coast there were just two passengers and three crewmen left alive.[6]

Within four months of the attack on Pearl Harbor the Japanese had achieved most of their war aims; they had captured Malaya and Singapore, the entire Dutch East Indies and most of the American-governed Philippine archipelago. The remaining American footholds in the Philippines were not destined to resist much longer. It was imperative for the Japanese that what had been seized should be held while the American will to resist was broken. In addition a successful thrust westwards towards the Middle East and a junction with the German forces would place the Allies in an untenable position. It is perhaps fortunate for the Allies that the Japanese had their eyes firmly fixed on the Pacific, where the

The Dutch merchant ship Rooseboom, *sunk by the Japanese submarine* I-59.

Americans were rightly regarded as the primary enemy, and that consequently the Indian Ocean was seen as a side show; greater co-operation with their German allies was not considered to be the strategic opportunity that it might have been.

As far as Japanese strategy was concerned their next large submarine sortie into the Indian Ocean, in June and July 1942 in the Mozambique Channel, fits the pattern of an isolated episode undertaken to pay lip service to their German and Italian allies while major operations where undertaken against the Americans in the Pacific. For this they detached the 1st Division of the 8th Submarine Flotilla, under Rear Admiral Noboru Ishizaki, previously based at Kwajalein in the Marshall Islands.

As a result, on Emperor Hirohito's birthday on 29 April 1942 a group of four Japanese submarines sailed from Penang for attacks against Allied shipping in the Indian Ocean; a fifth boat had sailed earlier. The Admiral, in accordance with Japanese custom, was embarked in one of the submarines specially built to carry a flotilla commander and his staff, on this occasion the *I-10*. The rest of his command consisted of the *I-16, I-18, I-20* and *I-30*. They were all much alike: the *I-16, I-18* and *I-20* displaced 2,554 tons (surface), had a surface speed of $23\frac{1}{2}$ knots and carried one midget submarine each. The *I-10* was a rather larger boat while the *I-30* was similar in size to the other three; however, these last two carried a small aircraft apiece. All five mounted a 140mm (5.5 inch) gun.

The midget submarines had a length of 78 feet, a diameter of 6 feet and a submerged displacement of only 46 tons. They carried a crew of two. They were designed to be taken into the operational area by a specially modified surface ship or parent submarine and consequently there was no means of recharging the batteries. This in turn limited their range to eighteen miles at their maximum submerged speed of 19 knots or, more practically, to eighty miles at 6 knots. There were two torpedo tubes, loaded from the 'muzzle' end. Five of these midgets had been used in the attack on Pearl Harbor; all had been lost and they had failed to achieve any success.

Also part of Admiral Ishizaki's force, though sailing independently, were the two armed merchant cruisers *Hokoku Maru* and *Aikoku Maru*. They were to be available to fuel the submarines when required and also to act as surface raiders.

The *I-30* (Commander Shinobu Endo) sailed a few days in advance and arrived off Aden at dusk on 7 May. There she catapulted her aircraft to reconnoitre the harbour during twilight. The process was repeated the next day over the French harbour of Djibouti, and then again at Zanzibar and Dar-es-Salaam on the 19th. No suitable targets – which to the Japanese meant warships – were seen at any of these ports. Meanwhile, the other four submarines followed a more southerly course across the Indian Ocean from Penang. On 20 May the *I-10*'s (Commander Y. Kayahara) aircraft flew over Durban at dawn, gave the wrong

The submarine I-26, *the same class as the* I-30 *which was part of Admiral Ishizaki's group. Note the hangar forward of the conning tower and the gun aft. Inset is Vice Admiral Mitsumi Shimizu, C-in-C of the 6th Fleet (Submarine Force) at the outbreak of war. (National Institute for Defence Studies, Tokyo (NIDS)*

Rear Admiral Noburo Ishizaki, whose submarine group carried out the attack on British ships in Diego Suarez. (NIDS)

reply when challenged, and disappeared out to sea without any action being taken. No attack was made by the submarine, although at that time there was a daily average of about forty merchant ships lying in the open roadstead off the port.

On the evening of the 29th the *I-10* was off Diego Suarez in Madagascar and once again launched her aircraft at dusk. It was detected and the battleship HMS *Ramillies* changed her berth as a matter of security, but the exploit was credited to a French aircraft from the south of the island.[7] As with the earlier reconnaissance over Aden and Durban, no thought seems to have been given to the possibility that the planes might have been Japanese. It was a clear moonlit night and the submarine's aircraft reported a battleship, a cruiser and other ships at anchor in the bay. The Japanese Admiral gave this information to the *I-16, I-18* and *I-20* and ordered them to close the entrance of the harbour and begin the attack.

The *I-20* (Commander T. Yamada) was the first to launch her midget, crewed by Lieutenant Saburo Akieda and Petty Officer Masami Takemoto, some nine miles from the approaches to the harbour at Diego Suarez. A few miles away, Sub Lieutenant Maoji Iwase and Petty Officer Takazo Takata similarly headed for the harbour in a midget launched from the *I-16* (Commander K. Yamada). The *I-18* had damaged her engines and this had left her too far away to be able to take part in the operation. Inside the harbour the old battleship *Ramillies*, having been

The Wantabe E9W1 floatplane – called SLIM by the Americans – was brought into service in 1936 and used by submarines on blockade patrols off the China coast but was obsolete by 1941. It took twenty minutes to assemble the plane on the deck of the submarine after surfacing, after which it was catapulted off. On return from its reconnaissance the aircraft landed alongside the submarine, was hoisted aboard and then dismantled for stowage in the hangar requiring the submarine to be surfaced for a considerable time. (Norman Polmar)

The E14Y1 single wing floatplane, known as the Glen, became operational at the end of 1940. It could be assembled and readied for flight in only 10 minutes but otherwise had all the disadvantages of the E9W1 in requiring the submarine to be surfaced for long periods during launch and recovery. It had a maximum speed of 190 knots and a range of 570 miles. (Norman Polmar)

Midget submarine of the type used in the attack on HMS Ramillies *in Diego Suarez. (NIDS)*

steaming in monotonous circles all day after the air alert the previous evening, dropped anchor near to the position she had originally occupied. Close by was a destroyer and HMS *Karanja*, an assault landing ship.[8] Nearer the harbour entrance was the tanker *British Loyalty*, while at a quay was another ship, fully laden with ammunition.

Suddenly, at about 8.15 p.m., the quiet of the evening in the great harbour was shattered when the battleship was hit on the port side by a single torpedo from the Lieutenant Akieda's midget. About an hour later the *British Loyalty* was also hit by a single torpedo from the same submarine as she tried to get underway. The torpedo hit the tanker in the engine room as she was going astern from her berth. Whether the torpedo was intended for the tanker or the battleship will never be known.

A second hit may well have sunk the *Ramillies*; as it was, she was out of action for twelve months. The *British Loyalty* was left with her stern on the bottom but was later salvaged. The existence of the ammunition ship at the quay was unknown to the Japanese and her destruction would have been catastrophic.

After its successes the midget submarine crewed by Lieutenant Saburo

Akieda and Petty Officer Masami Takemoto ran aground on a reef as it was leaving harbour. Both men abandoned the craft and tried to make their way overland to a rendezvous from where they would be picked up. The Japanese submarines waited for three days at the rendezvous position searching for any sign of their comrades, but in vain. The two men who had escaped were found by a British Commando patrol; they refused to surrender and were killed. Akieda's report of the operation was found on his body. Today the site is marked by a plaque inscribed: 'Ici Sont Morts le 3 Juin Deux Officers Marins Japonais d'un Sous-Marin de Poche'. The fate of the second midget is not known.

The *Hokoku Maru* and *Aikoku Maru* were on hand, in a position 600 miles south east of Madagascar, to provide fuel and supplies for the submarines. The two ships had sailed in company across the Indian Ocean but their only victim had been the Dutch tanker *Genota*, which had been captured early in May and sent to Singapore with a prize crew. After fuelling the submarines these two ships opened Admiral Ishizaki's assault on the Mozambique Channel on 5 June 1942, when they sank the 6,757 ton British cargo-passenger liner *Elysia*, a veteran of the First World War. Survivors were picked up by a hospital ship the next day. The two raiders then moved deeper into the Indian Ocean and a month later they sank their next – and last – victim, the British motor vessel *Hauraki*, before returning to Singapore.

Admiral Ishizaki, having blooded his Division on a real battleship and ensured that they were topped up with fuel, sent two submarines to each end of the Mozambique Channel to attack merchant shipping. The fifth boat, the *I-30*, was detached round the Cape of Good Hope. After a long voyage she entered the port of Lorient, on the coast of the Bay of Biscay, on 5 August with an escort of German minesweepers.

Between 5 June and 9 July, when Ishizaki ordered his boats back to Penang, the *I-10* sank eight merchant ships while the *I-18* (Commander K. Otani), which also operated in the southern part of the Channel, sank three ships. At the same time the *I-16* and *I-20*, in the northern part of the Channel, sank three and seven ships respectively. None of the survivors from these vessels suffered the calculated brutality that later became the hallmark of the actions of many Japanese submarine commanding officers.

The passage of the *I-30* to France has already been recorded. A month later, when she had been loaded with equipment and technical material, such as radar, rocket and glider bombs, she sailed for Singapore. On 13 October she left Singapore for Japan but, when only three miles east of the port, she was mined and sunk. Thirteen of her crew were killed and all the valuable cargo was lost.

The next submarine to sail for France was the *I-8* (Captain Shinji Uchino)

An overhead view of the Japanese submarine I-8 arriving in Lorient from the Far East on 6 July 1943. Note the unusual twin 5.5 inch gun mounting forward of the conning tower. (RN Submarine Museum)

on 6 July 1943. She carried not only her own crew but also a crew for the *U-1224*, which was to be handed over to the Japanese Navy as the *RO-501*. This type IXC submarine of 1,120 tons surface displacement was one of two that Hitler had ordered to be given to the Japanese as a model of German submarines. Vice Admiral Shigeru Fukutome, the Chief of Staff to the Admiral commanding the Combined Fleet, was not impressed by the gift – which he had not seen – and thought that the boat would be of little value to the Japanese Navy, as was probably reflected in the allocation of a 'RO' number.

The German *U-161* met with the *I-8* off the Azores and transferred a liaison officer and an aircraft search radar for protection during the hazardous transit of the Bay of Biscay. After a sixty-one day voyage the Japanese crews found themselves safely in the German occupied port of Lorient. For the return trip the submarine was loaded with technical torpedo and gunnery machinery before setting off on 5 October. In the South Atlantic the submarine was surprised and bombed by an aircraft but sustained no serious damage. Despite this clear indication of Allied patrols she made several radio transmissions to her base, some

The crew of the I-8 being entertained by German submariners at a French chateau which had been requisitioned as a shore accommodation for crews resting between patrols. (RN Submarine Museum)

of which were picked up in South Africa. With luck very much on her side, she escaped further attention and reached Singapore some sixty-four days later. She then went on to reach Japan safely, the only submarine to do the double trip successfully.

The crew of the *RO-501* took some time to become acquainted with the German design, and it was May 1944 before she sailed from Hamburg for her new home. In mid-Atlantic she met with the American destroyer *Francis M. Robinson* and was sunk with no survivors.

In November 1943 the *I-29* (Commander T. Kinashi) sailed from Penang en route for Europe. She met with a German supply ship in the South Indian Ocean and took onboard extra fuel for the long passage. In spite of the fact that the British and Americans had vital information about her progress from 'Ultra',[9] it was not practicable to act on the information without risk of its compromise and the *I-29* arrived safely at Lorient in German occupied France. The scientists and specialists she carried were disembarked and her cargo of raw materials for Germany was unloaded. For the return to Japan she was loaded with important German scientific equipment and blueprints of new and secret weapons, including the latest Messerschmitt fighter aircraft, the Me163 and Me262. Like the *I-8* before her she arrived back in Singapore to refuel before starting the final stage of her voyage to Japan, but unlike the *I-8* that final stage was never completed; on 26 July 1944, while south of Formosa (now Taiwan), she was sighted by the USS *Sawfish* (Lieutenant Commander Alan Banister) and sent to the bottom with no survivors.

Although many of the plans for both the new Messerschmitt aircraft went to the bottom of the South China Sea with the *I-29*, the Japanese went ahead with their intention to build the rocket powered Me163, and the task was given to Mitsubishi Shusui. Two prototype aircraft were eventually produced, one each for the Army and the Navy. Only the naval version was flown before the end of the war and that crashed during a test flight in July 1945.

Following closely behind the *I-29*, the *I-34* also left Singapore for France in November 1943. Her fate off Penang at the hands of HMS *Taurus* is related elsewhere.[10] The last of the Japanese submarines to attempt a cargo carrying run to Europe was the *I-52*. She was returning to the Far East when, on 24 June 1944, she was caught and sunk off the Azores by aircraft from the US aircraft carrier *Bogue*.

The *I-29* had previously been involved in a rare example of German-Japanese co-operation. In late April 1943 the submarine had effected a rendezvous with the *U-180* (*Korvettenkapitan* Werner Musenberg) some 600 miles east of Durban. In weather conditions that must have made boatwork between the two submarines extremely difficult and hazardous, the U-boat transferred the Indian Nationalist leader, Subhas Chandra Bose, and Abid

Hasan, an anti-British Arab fanatic. In addition the Germans had sent their allies plans of new weapons and a sample consignment of 'Bolde' – a chemical device which when released by a submarine would produce a mass of bubbles to confuse the enemy's asdic. In return the U-boat took onboard three of the latest Japanese torpedoes, two boxes of gold, some quinine and two Japanese officers, the whole operation taking several days to complete. The *U-180* made a successful voyage back to its French base while the *I-29* landed Chandra Bose in Singapore. He subsequently became the leader of the Indian National Army which recruited from the ranks of Indian POWs.[11] Several Indians of the I.N.A. were trained in sabotage at Penang and it was planned that they were to be landed in India by a Japanese submarine. The first group left Penang in December 1943 and were landed on the coast between Bombay and Karachi. The mission ended in farce when, after wandering ineffectually for two months, the potential saboteurs surrendered to the police.

When the *I-26* (Lieutenant Commander T. Kusaka) left Penang in February 1944 a much more ambitious operation was planned. Onboard the submarine were twenty-two Indians of the I.N.A. who were to be landed on the coast of what is now Pakistan, from where they were to travel to the North West Frontier region before beginning their subversive operations. The men were fortunate to reach their landing area at all, because the submarine was sighted by HMS *Storm* soon after leaving Penang but an attack was not possible, as the Japanese boat fortuitously zigzagged away just before the *Storm* was ready to fire. The Muslims among the I.N.A. party were insulted that the Japanese submariners treated them with disdain, even serving them pork with their meals. Kusaka successfully put the men ashore at the second attempt, whereupon the whole party surrendered to the Police. Even more incredible is the fact that in the weeks prior to their departure they had been carefully indoctrinated immediately to offer themselves for surrender by the officer responsible for their training, Captain Mahmood Khan Durrani, who had, in fact, remained loyal to the British. When the failure of this mission became known Captain Durrani was interrogated and badly treated by the Japanese military police, the *Kempetai*. In 1945, when the British re-occupied Malaya Captain Durrani was found in prison and subsequently awarded the George Cross.

An order issued on 20 March 1943 by Rear Admiral Takero Kouta, the Commander of the Japanese First Submarine Force at Truk, included the following instruction to submarine commanders:

> *Do not stop at the sinking of enemy ships and cargoes. At the same time carry out the complete destruction of the crews of the enemy ship.*

Simply to quote this order – which was apparently obeyed at whim by commanding officers – does not explain or excuse the incidences of brutality to the crews of torpedoed merchant ships. Most of the cases where this did happen were in the Indian Ocean, but not exclusively so. The treatment doled out to Allied POWs is well documented, and is often explained by reference to the Japanese code of honour, *Gyokusai*, which forbade a serviceman to surrender and made him regard those that did as having no honour – or value. The centuries old world-wide law of the sea requiring seamen to aid others in distress, was deliberately ignored.

Perhaps the most infamous of the Japanese submarine commanding officers was Commander Tatsunosuke Ariizumi, who had taken over the *I-8* after she had returned from her record breaking trip to France and back. His first victim was the 5,787 ton Dutch steamer *Tjisalak*. She was an old ship, built in 1917, and had spent most of her life in the Dutch East Indies until February 1942, when she escaped from Java only hours ahead of the invading enemy. In the next two years she sailed safely with many Atlantic convoys before returning to eastern waters. Early on 26 March 1944 she was sailing independently between Melbourne and Colombo and was within 500 miles of her destination when she was struck by two torpedoes just abaft the bridge on the port side. On fire, listing badly and obviously sinking, she was abandoned. Three of the crew had been killed by the explosions but all the remainder were able to reach the lifeboats and life-rafts.

The *I-8* surfaced about 100 yards from the pathetic group of survivors. Gestures from the Japanese crew brought the lifeboats alongside and the Dutch Captain, along with eight others from the first boat, was ordered onboard and up to the conning tower. Next, all the rest were ordered aboard, and after being stripped of their lifebelts and anything of value they were sent forward on the casing. Then they were taken aft individually, beaten with hammers and shot as they fell overboard. Ninety-eight passengers and crew were killed. Surprisingly, five men escaped the slaughter and managed to reach one of the drifting lifeboats while Ariizumi took the *I-8* off to look for fresh targets.

Two days later the hopes of the five men were raised when a ship was sighted approaching them. To their horror they were again shelled, though mercifully without causing further casualties. The American liberty ship *James A Wilder* had thought their lifeboat was the conning tower of a partially surfaced submarine and had taken no chances.

On 30 March Ariizumi struck again. Two torpedoes brought the *City of Adelaide* to a stop, the stricken ship subsequently being sent to the bottom after being hit by gunfire. If Ariizumi had used the orders of Admiral Kouta as an excuse for his actions after sinking the *Tjisalak* on the 26th, those very same orders were thankfully ignored just four days later.

Commander Tatsunosuke Ariizumi, the notorious Commanding Officer of the I-8. *(Captain B. Edwards)*

The *Nellore* was another victim of Ariizumi's *I-8*, and the story told by her survivors is quite different. The ship was torpedoed and sunk on 29 June 1944 with about 150 out of the 240 onboard reaching the comparative safety of the lifeboats. Some of the passengers were convinced that they had been sunk by a German U-boat, as instructions were passed in a German accent by a 'courteous white submariner', while the ship's officers stated that they had heard 'guttural (*sic*) Japanese orders.' The only unusual action was to deprive all those in one lifeboat of their lifebelts. The submarine then left the area to seek another victim. One lifeboat eventually reached Madagascar with only 11 out of the original 47 onboard still alive. The survivors from another lifeboat were rescued and taken to Diego Garcia.

The 7,176 ton Liberty Ship *Jean Nicolet* sailed from Fremantle for Colombo on 21 June 1944. On 2 July she was sighted by the *I-8* and shortly after 7.00 p.m. she was hit by two of a salvo of three torpedoes. The ship immediately took a heavy list to starboard but all 100 men onboard managed to board the 4 lifeboats and rafts that could be launched. No sooner was this done than shells began to slam into the sinking ship, setting her on fire. Whether the timing was deliberate or accidental is not known.

The survivors, illuminated by a powerful searchlight, were ordered onboard the submarine and, as before, were stripped of their lifejackets and personal possessions before being bound with their hands behind their backs. The unfortunate seamen were then taken aft and made to 'run the gauntlet' as they were struck with hammers and other weapons before being shot and pushed into the sea. Before all the men had been killed, alarm bells sounded within the submarine and the *I-8* dived.

HMIS *Hoxa* eventually picked up a mere twenty-three survivors.

Ariizumi may have become the most notorious of the Japanese submariners operating in the Indian Ocean[12] but he was not the first to follow the orders of Admiral Kouta. On 14 December 1943 the *Daisy Moller* was on passage from Colombo to Chittagong when she was hit by a single torpedo fired from the *RO-110* under the command of Lieutenant Kazuro Ebato. The ship soon took on a massive list to starboard, which made launching the lifeboats even more difficult for a crew who had suddenly been roused from sleep in the dark hour before dawn. Nevertheless, the whole crew managed to get away. Land was only about three miles off and they were comforted to know that the Wireless Operator had sent a distress signal.

However, the real ordeal of the *Daisy Moller*'s crew was only just about to begin. Ebato surfaced the submarine, rammed the lifeboats and then machine gunned the survivors as they struggled to save themselves. Out of the seventy-one men who had abandoned the ship before she sank, fifty-five were left face down in a blood-stained sea. The remainder managed to reach the shore after Ebato took his boat seawards to seek other targets.

It was two months before Ebato had the chance to add to his score. South of the Indian port of Vizgapatam, he sighted a small convoy and altered course to attack. His first torpedo damaged the steamer *Asphalion* but the escort was almost immediately in contact with the submarine. A series of attacks by the Australian minesweepers *Ipswich* and *Launceston* and the Indian sloop *Jumma* sent the submarine to the bottom with all hands.

The *I-37* was also at sea in the Indian Ocean in February 1944. The submarine's commanding officer was Lieutenant Commander H. Nakagawa who, when in command of the *I-177* in March 1943, had brutally attacked the hospital ship *Centaur* off Brisbane. Nearly a year later, on the 22 February 1944, when 300 miles west of Adu Atoll, southernmost of the Maldive Islands, the *I-37* met with the bulk grain carrier *British Chivalry* which was on passage from Melbourne to Abadan. Two torpedoes were fired at the British ship. The first missed astern but the second hit the ship on the starboard side, in the engine room. Six of the crew were killed by the explosion but the remaining fifty-one abandoned ship into the two lifeboats that had been launched. The *I-37* then proceeded to finish off the tanker. Some twenty

Survivors of the merchant ship Sutlej *being rescued by HMS* Flamingo. *Eighteen men were picked up from two of these rafts almost seven weeks after the ship had been sunk. (Captain B. Edwards)*

rounds from the 140mm gun were fired, of which only three hit the target before the ship was finally sunk by another torpedo. Nakagawa then set about the lifeboats and the survivors, firing machine guns into them until he believed that all were killed. When the submarine finally left the area it was found that the casualties were not as high as might have been expected; only thirteen killed and five wounded. It was another thirty-seven days before the survivors were picked up by the British motor vessel *Delane*.

On 26 February Nakagawa struck again. The *Sutlej* was sunk after being hit by just one torpedo, going down in under four minutes. After questioning the survivors in the lifeboats about their cargo and destination the machine gunners again opened fire. The submarine remained in the area for about an hour before sailing away in search of other targets. HMS *Solvra* picked up just five survivors, who had travelled 1,300 miles in forty-one days onboard one of the boats. Two rafts with eighteen more survivors were picked up by HMS *Flamingo* a week later.

Three days later the *Ascot* was Nakagawa's next victim. After what had become Nakagawa's habitual savagery seven men dragged themselves aboard the remaining life-raft to watch the eventual sinking of their ship as the *I-37* disappeared into the darkness. These survivors were lucky to be picked up the following day by the Dutch ship *Straat Soenda*.

The reign of terror was not yet over, though the *I-37* had returned to Penang. In mid-March the *Nancy Moller* fell victim to the *I-165*, commanded by Lieutenant T. Shimizu. Two torpedoes struck the old collier, a sister ship of the *Daisy Moller*, which had earlier been sunk by the *RO-110*. A total of thirty-two of the ship's crew of sixty-five died in the massacre that followed the collier's sinking, while one of the gun's crew, who alone had been taken onboard the submarine, survived starvation and brutality as a POW to be released at the end of the war. The *I-165* sank no more ships on that patrol and in June was herself sunk by American naval aircraft in the Pacific, although Lieutenant Shimizu was not onboard at the time.

A final atrocity occurred when the *I-26* sank the 7,000 ton Liberty Ship *Richard Hovey* at the end of March 1944. She left Bombay bound for the USA via Aden, and two days out she met the Japanese submarine. Lieutenant Commander Kusaka hit with two out of the three torpedoes he fired. A fourth

Survivors of the Nancy Moller *being picked up by a whaler from the cruiser HMS* Emerald. *(Captain B. Edwards)*

torpedo later finished the ship off before the submarine surfaced to fire on the survivors. Eventually the submarine disappeared into the growing darkness, towing the only undamaged lifeboat and leaving the survivors to fend for themselves as best they could. There was little or no fresh water and no fuel for the engines of the damaged lifeboats. After fifteen days thirty-eight survivors in one boat were picked up by another merchant ship, a second boat with twenty-four men onboard having been picked up a few days earlier. Kusaka's attempts to kill the survivors were singularly ineffective as not one man perished during the attack on the lifeboats, yet there is no doubt that opening fire on the lifeboats was in itself an act against all the rules of the sea. Incidentally, the lifeboat towed from the scene of the sinking had to be cast adrift by Kusaka, but only when the *I-26* was a sufficient distance away from the survivors so that they could not make use of it.[13]

Admiral Sir James Somerville, the Commander in Chief of the Eastern Fleet, was concerned by the possible effect of these atrocities on the morale of Allied merchant seamen – perhaps something that the Japanese themselves hoped for. Steps were taken to try to prevent news of the sinkings and the massacres that followed becoming public knowledge. Even so, many merchant seamen were well aware of what had happened, as were their military colleagues. An official protest, made through the Swiss Government and subsequently conveyed to the Japanese, fell on deaf ears.

On 5 February 1944 convoy KR8 sailed from Kilindini in Kenya for Colombo with troop reinforcements and other service personnel. The convoy consisted of the merchant ships *Ekma, Ellenga, City of Paris, Varsova* and the Commodore's ship the *Khedive Ismail*. The first four ships were in two columns, the *Khedive Ismail* sailing slightly ahead and between the columns. The original close escort of a corvette and two ex-United States' coastguard cutters left the convoy after two days, leaving only the old cruiser HMS *Hawkins* to watch over the ships until the arrival of two modern destroyers from Colombo.

At first light on the 12th the new escort, in the form of HMS *Petard* and *Paladin*, joined the convoy and took station on either bow at a distance of four to six miles, circling and zigzagging as they searched for any submarines. The afternoon watchman had scarcely closed up in the *Petard* when the cry went up: 'Periscope bearing red 150.' As the crew scrambled to action stations the ship increased to full speed and turned under full helm towards the sighting. At the same time there was a massive underwater explosion and a huge sheet of flame and a cloud of black smoke rose from the after part of the *Khedive Ismail*. She had been struck by two torpedoes out of a salvo of four fired from the *I-27* (Lieutenant Commander Toshiaki Fukumura). Both had hit on the starboard side in the vicinity of the boiler and engine rooms, leaving the troop ship on

A submarine of the RO-110 *class. (NIDS)*

her beam ends in less than a minute. Within three minutes the bow rose from the sea, exposing a length of the keel, before she rapidly slipped stern first beneath the waves.

The recorded number of those onboard varies somewhat depending on which report of the disaster is read, but it is generally accepted that there were about 1,500 men and women, including the crew.[14] The high casualty list arose from the speed at which the ship sank and the fact that many of the troops were attending a concert below decks.

In accordance with instructions, the Senior Officer of the escort in HMS *Hawkins* ordered the four remaining ships to 'scatter', the cruiser going with them towards a preplanned rendezvous position. This was hardly noticed at the time on the *Petard*'s bridge as the asdic team gained contact with the *I-27*. It fell to the destroyer's Captain, Lieutenant Commander Rupert Egan, to make an agonising decision. The submarine was positioned under a group of survivors who were vainly swimming in the water, thinking the destroyer was coming to pick them up. This fact made the explosion of the pattern of eight depth charges seem all the more violent. It was left to the *Paladin* to try and rescue as many as possible from the water as Egan directed his ship into two more deliberate attacks on the submarine.

After the third attack the submarine surfaced almost in the middle of the explosions, damaged but still able to fight. The Japanese made suicidally brave attempts to man their 140mm deck gun but to no avail, and they eventually gave up when the gun itself was damaged. By then the *Paladin* had picked up just 214 survivors from the troop ship. She tried to ram the submarine but was ordered off by Egan just in time, as the possible resultant damage to the destroyer could have sunk her. Even so, she passed so close to the submarine that its hydroplane ripped a hole along her hull.

The 4-inch guns of the two destroyers, firing shell with DA fuses (Direct Action – exploding on hitting), could make no impression on the hull of the Japanese submarine. The only ship with guns capable of firing armour piercing shell was the *Hawkins*, and by then she was miles away. The submarine was obviously damaged so she could not dive, her periscopes were probably damaged so she could not see; however, she could still fire torpedoes if it were thought the destroyers were ahead or astern. The destroyer's guns could maim her no further and it looked like a stand off. Egan tried passing close to the submarine and firing depth charges set to explode at a shallow depth, but this did not work. A plan was devised to put a boarding party on to the submarine's casing and place an explosive charge against the hull, but this idea had to be discarded as impracticable. There was only one possible solution remaining.

Each destroyer was fitted with eight torpedoes. The laid down drill was for these to be fired in one or two salvos but, for some reason never explained, Egan decided to fire a single torpedo at his target, which was now proceeding on a calm sea on a steady course and with a speed of about 5 knots. Perhaps he did not wish to waste these precious weapons. In any event, the first missed. So did the second, and the third. And the fourth, the fifth and the sixth. With bated breath the seventh was fired – and the submarine disappeared in a column of water and flame. Remarkably, a single Japanese sailor was left alive in the water, marking the spot where the *I-27* had been; he allowed himself to be picked up by the *Petard*.

The survivors from the *Khedive Ismail* were transferred from the damaged *Paladin* and then the two destroyers made their way to the British base at Adu Atoll. With the sinking of the Japanese *I-27* the *Petard* completed a unique trio of victories by managing to sink a submarine from each of the Axis powers. In September 1942 she was part of a force that had sunk the German *U-559* and in December that same year she sank the Italian *Uarsciek*.

March 1944 was the last month in which Japanese submarines had a marked effect in the Indian Ocean. The relatively few sinkings were almost entirely the work of the German U-boats. Commander Ariizumi sank the *Jean Nicolet* (already described) in July, while the *RO-113* (Lieutenant Kiyoshi Harada) claimed two ships sunk and one damaged in November and December. At the end of December the *RO-113* and *RO-114* returned from patrol to Penang, and this marked the end of Japanese submarine operations in the Indian Ocean. All their remaining boats were required in the more important areas in the Pacific.

Considering the large number of ships sailing across the Indian Ocean, many of them unescorted, it was hardly a successful campaign. Submarines had been at sea for long periods without seeing a target. Compared to the successes of the American boats operating against the Japanese lines of communication, the Japanese submariners had failed dismally; compared to the patrols by the British and Dutch boats off the Malay coast, the Japanese had certainly not made the impact on the war at sea that might have been expected.

Notes:

1 *Naval Weapons of World War Two* by John Campbell (Conway 1985). The excellence of Japanese torpedoes was due to the use of pure oxygen instead of air in the propulsion system. The submarine torpedo in use from 1938 had a range of 9,000 yards at 50 knots, far in excess of any weapon used by the British or Americans.

2 Japanese naval ranks are *Tai-sho* (Admiral), *Chu-sho* (Vice-Admiral), *Sho-Sho* (Rear Admiral), *Tai-sa* (Captain), *Chu-sa* (Commander) and *Sho-sa* (Lieutenant Commander). For ease of reading the British equivalents have been used in this narrative.

3 Surviving Japanese submarines numbered from *I-51* to *I-85* had their numbers changed in May 1942 by adding 100; new construction submarines were then allocated the smaller numbers.

4 Another source states that the *I-5* went aground on a reef while leaving Sterling Bay and was salvaged in the latter part of March.

5 A catapult fitted along the forward casing of the submarine enabled the seaplane to become airborne. However, it had to land on the sea and manoeuvre alongside the submarine before being hoisted aboard by a crane. This involved the submarine remaining on the surface for about twenty minutes.

6 *The Boat* by Walter Gibson (Merritt & Hatcher 1952) tells the full story of the sinking of this ship and the terrible voyage that followed.

7 Some sources continue the myth that this aircraft was from a French submarine, ignoring the fact that the only French submarine with an aircraft capability had been sunk in the West Indies in February 1942.

8 One of the ships of the British assault force.

9 'Ultra Top Secret' was the classification given to messages containing intelligence gained by the decryption of German and Italian codes, the word 'Ultra' has subsequently been used to describe all aspects of this form of Signal Intelligence. With the outbreak of the war against Japan the same codeword was used to include all Japanese communications broken by crypto-analysis. 'Magic' was the codeword given by the Americans for decoded Japanese diplomatic communications.

10 See Chapter Nine.

11 Bose was killed in an air crash in Formosa in 1945 and his INA never became an effective force for the Japanese.

12 Commander Ariizumi was never tried for war crimes, but died by his own hand. At the end of the war he was commanding the large (3,530 tons surfaced/6,560 tons submerged) submarine *I-400*, capable of carrying three aircraft to raid as far afield as the Panama Canal. The submarine had sailed for its first operational patrol just before the end of the war and with the Japanese surrender Ariizumi was ordered to return to Japan. As the submarine was entering Tokyo Bay Commander Ariizumi shot himself.

13 The PRO holds detailed accounts of survivors from merchant ships, 1939-45, under reference ADM199/2130-48.

14 Detail supplied to the author by the Naval Historical Branch of the MOD.

Six

The Americans and the Loss of the USS *Grenadier*

At the time of the Japanese attack on the United States at Pearl Harbor in December 1941 there were 55 large and 18 medium-sized submarines operational in the Asiatic and Pacific Fleets out of a total of 111 in the whole of the US Navy. In addition there were a further 73 submarines under construction.[1] During the First World War the United States had based a squadron of 'L' class submarines in Ireland where they operated with the Royal Navy. It was an unrewarding deployment with few opportunities for attack and it ended with not a single sinking being credited to an American submarine. However, American submarines were to become a decisive weapon in the Pacific campaigns of 1942-45, destroying over sixty per cent of all Japanese merchant shipping and accounting for nearly a third of all Japanese warship losses.[2]

Pre-war training for American submariners concentrated on the fact that the primary function of the submarine was to attack enemy heavy ships – a heavy ship being defined as a battleship, battle cruiser or aircraft carrier. It was anticipated that there would be times when this task would be specially extended to include cruisers or even other types of warship.[3] Attacks on merchant shipping were not considered as these were thought to be impracticable under the provisions of International Law. Like the British and the Germans, the Americans had accepted the provisions of article 22 of the 1930 London Naval Treaty, which placed restrictions on the actions of submarines in the event of war by the imposition of 'Prize Rules'. However, by December 1941 German and British submarines were each waging war without restriction on the other's merchant ships, which were carrying vital supplies. Given the circumstances of the Japanese attack at Pearl Harbor, and with the German and British precedent, it is hardly surprising that an immediate order was issued to American forces: 'Execute unrestricted submarine and air warfare against Japan.'

Having trained for the task of operating with the American battle fleet and against the Japanese heavy ships, this new edict was totally unexpected by American submarine commanders. The new strategy, combined with the fact that, like the Germans, American torpedoes were running deeper than the set depth when fitted with warheads, may account for the fact that American submariners achieved little during the opening months of the war and singularly failed to interrupt the Japanese landings in either the Philippines or the Dutch East Indies. In addition, the Americans also had to contend with serious flaws in the magnetic firing pistols in the warheads.

When the Japanese attacked the Cavite Naval Base in Manila Bay on 10 December the submarine *Sealion* was in dock being refitted. Nearby was the *Seadragon* which had almost finished an overhaul. In the second wave of attacks two bombs hit the *Sealion*, one at the after end of the conning tower, the other penetrating into the engine room near the hatch. The submarine was left badly damaged and listing; the stern sank to the bottom and the hull began to fill with water. Four men were killed. Fragments of the stricken submarine and bomb splinters gashed holes in the *Seadragon*'s conning tower where one officer was killed and several ratings were wounded. The five fatal casualties on the two boats were the first American submariners to be killed in the war. Elsewhere the bombs had turned Cavite into a shambles, destroying valuable repair facilities and torpedo stocks. The *Seadragon*, with fires raging and her steering damaged, was towed away for emergency repairs before being sent to Surabaya where the Dutch were able to make her ready for war. The *Sealion* was considered beyond repair and was destroyed with three depth charges on Christmas Day.

By the following day, twenty-two of the surviving twenty-eight submarines of the American Asiatic Fleet had left for patrol. One of these was the *Seawolf* (SS-197) under the command of Lieutenant Commander Freddie Warder. The Japanese seaplane tender *Sanyo Maru* was attacked by the *Seawolf* off one of the Japanese landing beaches in northern Luzon; eight torpedoes were fired in two separate attacks, no hits were recorded although one torpedo is believed to have struck its target without exploding. It was an ominous start to what became a long running saga of torpedo failures.

With the capture of Cavite by the Japanese, the American submarines were ordered to Surabaya in Java, at a time when the Dutch were determined to prevent the Japanese reaching Java and Sumatra. However, the Australians wanted all forces to withdraw south of the Dutch island chain so that they could protect

Australia itself. The American view, as voiced by Admiral Thomas Hart, the Commander of the Asiatic Fleet, agreed with the Dutch that the Japanese should be stopped as soon as possible, while the British were already fully engaged with the Japanese in Malaya and had few naval forces available. Accordingly the American submarines were deployed to try and catch the Japanese invasion forces as well as running supply and evacuation missions to Bataan and Corregidor. Only later did they begin operations south of Java.

When the *Seawolf* sailed from the Dutch base in mid-February it was for her fourth war patrol, which was destined to be the most hectic. Two Japanese freighters were damaged by torpedoes on the 19th and a week later two more merchant ships with an escorting destroyer were attacked but without result. On 31 March Warder encountered a Japanese force of three light cruisers south of Java, near Christmas Island. His first attack was unsuccessful. The next day the *Seawolf* attacked twice more, achieving just one hit[4] on the cruiser *Naka* which, although it put the ship out of action for many months, was all that Warder had to show for his persistence. The attacks had all been made at short range but Warder was unable to explain his lack of success, made all the more galling by the severe depth charging to which the *Seawolf* had been subjected. It was one of many instances in which the professionalism and efficiency of American submariners was put in jeopardy by the unreliability of their torpedoes, a situation which was to endure for many months before the problem was eventually resolved.

With the invasion of Java and the loss of the Dutch bases in the East Indies, the remaining US Navy submarines of the Asiatic Fleet went to Australia. In place of the combined ABDA (American, British, Dutch and Australian) Command under General Sir Archibald Wavell as Supreme Commander, the Allies divided their responsibilities. The Royal Navy was assigned control of all naval forces in the Indian Ocean and the waters surrounding Sumatra and off the coast of west Malaya; similarly, the US Navy had control throughout the whole of the Pacific, including the waters around Australia and New Zealand. The US Navy submarines operated from Brisbane on the east coast of Australia, under Captain Ralph Christie, and from Fremantle on the west coast, first under Captain John Wilkes and then Rear Admiral Charles Lockwood. Both bases formed part of General Douglas MacArthur's South West Pacific Command. From Fremantle the submarines made the long passage up the Australian coast, through the Straits separating the islands of the now Japanese held Dutch East Indies and on to their patrol areas in the South China Sea.

In late April 1942 Lieutenant Commander William ('Bull') Wright's USS *Sturgeon* (SS-187) was returning from patrol when she was ordered to pick up some stranded British airmen from the port of Tjilatjap on the south coast of Java. The Executive Officer, Lieutenant Chester Nimitz Jr., actually landed in the Japanese occupied port but was unable to find the airmen and take them to safety.

The submarine returned to Fremantle. Lieutenant Nimitz was subsequently awarded a Silver Star, the medal being presented to him by his father, who was the Commander-in-Chief of the US Pacific Fleet.[5]

That same month Lieutenant Commander Hiram (Hi) Cassedy, recently appointed to command the USS *Searaven* (SS-196), was more successful and managed to rescue thirty-three Australians from Timor. Ensign George Cook swam ashore through heavy surf in an attempt to contact the soldiers but failed. Three nights later he swam ashore again and this time was able to help the men, who were suffering badly from malaria and dysentery, out to the submarine. No sooner was the *Searaven* clear of the coast when a fire broke out in the submarine, cutting off power to the motors and filling the boat with smoke. As the crew struggled to control the fire the submarine lay helpless on the surface, a perfect target for the Japanese. Cassedy's signal for assistance was answered by the *Snapper* (SS-185), which was returning from a forlorn mission to Corregidor, and the damaged submarine was taken in tow. Later the tow was passed to an Australian sloop and both submarines returned safely to Fremantle.

In November 1942 the *Searaven* patrolled off Christmas Island, some 200 nautical miles south of the western end of Java. It was not a particularly successful patrol, not because of any shortcomings on the part of the *Searaven* but because there was simply no Japanese shipping to be found. Two similar patrols were carried out by the *Thresher* (SS-200) which visited the island to seek any Japanese shipping before going on to patrol through the Sunda Strait and then off the north coast of Java.

Only one other American submarine was to operate in the Indian Ocean area during the war. The USS *Grenadier* (SS-210) was sent on a patrol off the west coast of Malaya in early 1943, during which she was lost following a lucky – or unlucky, depending upon how you view the odds – attack by a Japanese aircraft. Although well documented, the story of the courage and determination of her crew deserves to be retold.

The *Grenadier* was one of the *Tambor* class of submarines, construction of which began in January 1939, the *Grenadier* herself being commissioned in May 1941. These boats were considered at the time to be the ultimate in refinement and habitability, the last to be built to peacetime construction standards. Over 300 feet in length overall, they displaced 1,475 tons on the surface and 2,370 tons dived, and carried a massive armament of twenty-four torpedoes in ten tubes, six forward and four aft. The submarine's maximum surface speed was credited at 20 knots, and it had a range of 11,000 miles at 10 knots. The safe diving depth was 250 feet. The *Grenadier*, like all American submarines at that time, was built for service in the Pacific Ocean, where distances were huge and depth of water never a problem, and they may have been considered too big to have been sent to an area of confined and relatively shallow water such as was found off the west coast of

Malaya. Lieutenant Commander Edward Young RNVR, the Commanding Officer of HMS *Storm*, a submarine not much bigger than half the size of the *Grenadier*, said of these waters:[6]

> *In few places were there as much as forty fathoms of water, the ten fathom line would never be very far away…I had a feeling that the area would begin to seem very small if we ran into serious anti-submarine opposition.*

The USS *Grenadier* was lost on the morning of 22 April 1943. That much is known; as is the cause of her loss, for at the end of the war the survivors returned home to tell their story. The mystery begins when one considers that the *Grenadier* was lost in an area in which no other US submarine had previously been, and to which no other US submarine would go before the end of the war. The mystery deepens upon realisation that this was an area which had been the preserve of the British and Dutch submariners operating from Ceylon, and was to remain their domain for the rest of the war.

Under the command of Lieutenant Commander John A. Fitzgerald USN, the *Grenadier* had sailed from Fremantle on 20 March 1943 for her sixth war patrol. Her patrol area was to the north of the Malacca Straits, an area which, although comparatively free of Japanese shipping, was nevertheless considered to be of vital importance in the event of a British offensive in Burma because of the Japanese supply lines from Singapore. After sinking a small freighter off the island of Phuket on 6 April, Fitzgerald and his crew remained in the area for the next two weeks without a worthwhile target. So little was seen that Fitzgerald requested a move to more profitable waters.[7]

During the night of 20 April, and at the same time that Fitzgerald received fresh orders detailing the *Grenadier* for a patrol area off the Sunda Straits, two Japanese merchant ships were detected and Fitzgerald took the submarine to a point where he would be able to intercept them the following morning. Shortly before arriving in the position where he intended to submerge and wait for his quarry, Fitzgerald was forced to dive when the *Grenadier* was surprised by a Japanese aircraft.

The American lookouts were good and the submarine was quickly on her way down. As they passed 120 feet the Executive Officer remarked, 'We ought to be safe now!' – but they had not been quick enough, for even as he spoke the boat was rocked by an explosion. The force heeled her over 10° to 15°, all power and lights were lost and she came to rest on the bottom at about 270 feet. The hull and hatches were leaking badly in several places and there was a fire in the controls of the main motors. The next few hours were to bring considerably more internal damage to light.

Throughout the day the crew slaved to repair their boat. The fire was

Lieutenant Commander John Fitzgerald, the Commanding Officer of the USS Grenadier. *(US Navy)*

extinguished, a bucket chain kept the water from flooding the motors and men struggled to restore the propulsion.

At dusk the *Grenadier* was surfaced and the repair work continued. Both shafts were bent but eventually power was restored to one shaft to enable it be used at very slow speed, though even then it required a massive 2,750 amps instead of the normal 450 amps. They had no radio. An attempt to sail the submarine proved futile, as were efforts to take her nearer the coast so that the crew could be got ashore before she was scuttled. With the return of daylight more ships were sighted approaching and Fitzgerald decided to scuttle the boat, after destroying all his secret equipment and codes, and give his crew the best chance of survival that could be expected in the circumstances. However, before this could be put into operation another Japanese plane attacked. It was engaged with the submarine's two 20mm and two .30 inch machine guns, but another bomb dropped by the aircraft exploded close to the submarine, causing further damage. The attacker was hit and later crashed on landing at Penang.

With the approaching Japanese ships only some 1,800 yards away, the submarine's crew abandoned ship and the vents were opened to take her to the bottom. All eight officers and sixty-eight men were eventually picked up and taken to Penang. These men received brutal treatment from their Japanese captors until, in 1945, all but four of them were released from their prison camps.

So much for the 'how'. The 'why' is more complex, for few official papers have survived in public records. Those that do exist provide an intriguing insight into what may have happened, and reading between the lines has allowed the author to suggest an answer to the riddle of this lone American submarine patrol in the area to the North of the Malacca Straits.

First, it is necessary to go back to the Casablanca Conference (codenamed SYMBOL) in January 1943 where President Franklin D. Roosevelt, Prime Minister Winston Churchill and their respective Chiefs of Staff mapped out their strategy for the future course of the war. Most of the discussions centred on the need for the cross-Channel invasion of France and the way in which any future operations in the Mediterranean Theatre would be ordered after the expulsion of the Axis forces from the small area of North Africa which they then held. Of course, there was another war to be fought in the Far East against the Japanese, and decisions had to be taken for that Theatre as well.

The Americans, especially Admiral Ernest King and General George Marshall, were eager to allocate even more resources to fight the Japanese enemy while at the same time pressing for the Anglo-American invasion of France to be launched in the summer of 1943. Help for General Chiang Kai-shek, which it was hoped would tie down increasing numbers of Japanese troops in China, would entail greater effort by the British in Burma. The war in the Far East had seen British armies forced to capitulate in Singapore and retreat through Burma to the frontier with India. The recapture of Burma was an important objective for Churchill, though shortage of supplies, due to other fronts having higher priority, would mean that the Commanders in the Far East would have to do the best they could with what material they could obtain. Nevertheless, Operation ANAKIM, as the reconquest of Burma was then known, was agreed at Casablanca.

To this end, the Americans had agreed not only that British resources should be diverted from the build-up for the invasion of France but also that American assistance should be provided. In fact Admiral King, well known for his scornful hostility to all things British, had surprised his counterparts by offering them landing craft and escorts which they could use in the short term for operations in Burma.[8] That these resources were never actually used, or indeed even sent to the area, is another story.

Then, on 2 March 1943 Admiral King, as Commander in Chief of the US Navy (COMINCH), signalled the Admiralty in London[9] making two offers. Firstly, that two Australian based submarines from General MacArthur's Command would each make one patrol of three or four weeks duration in the area between Martaban (at the northern end of the Tenasserim Peninsular, Burma) and Malacca (on the West coast of Malaya, about 150 miles North of Singapore). Secondly, that six US submarines with their own depot ship would be based in Ceylon to operate under the Commander-in-Chief Eastern Fleet, Admiral Sir James Somerville, when the main operations got under way. King had reservations, for he noted that the shallow water off Martaban made close-in submarine operations unsuitable. He also commented that there were few targets in this area compared to the 'well stocked hunting grounds' where the US submarines were normally operating, and such a diversion of forces might actually be assisting the enemy.

In March 1943, when King made his offer of US support, the Anglo-Dutch submarine force in the Indian Ocean area consisted of just three operational boats, based in Ceylon. Of these the only British boat, HMS *Trusty*, had carried out a fifty-four day patrol in February which had taken her as far afield as Cambodia Point in French Indo-China, but she had been plagued with mechanical troubles during the patrol and she sailed for refit in the UK on 5 April. The other boats in the force were the Dutch O *21* and O *24*, the former being on patrol south of the *Grenadier* during mid-April, sinking a 7,000 ton Japanese merchant ship on 22 April[10] at the very time when the *Grenadier*'s crew were beginning their ordeal as POWs. A third Dutch submarine, the O *23*, was out of action with engine defects.

The die was cast. With the SYMBOL conference at Casablanca over, the Joint Chiefs of Staff in Washington signalled MacArthur on the 15 March[11] that he was to assign two submarines for one patrol each off the Martaban coast.

The result was that, only eighteen days after King's signal to London, the *Grenadier* sailed on her last patrol, the first of the two promised submarines from

The USS Grenadier. *(US Navy)*

General MacArthur's South West Pacific command. Before the *Grenadier* departed from Fremantle Captain 'Tex' McLean, the Squadron Commander, had protested this diversion of a valuable submarine from more fruitful hunting areas to one which was unlikely to show much result and furthermore was both confined and shallow.[12] McLean, unaware of the political overtones of this diversion, was naturally over-ruled. The extent to which Commander R.R. Helbert RN, the British Liaison Officer on the American Staff, was consulted, or indeed was privy to the background of this patrol, is not known.

It must be almost certain that the second patrol off the west coasts of Malaya and Thailand proposed by Admiral King was cancelled because of Fitzgerald's request for a move to a new area owing to a lack of targets and the subsequent loss of the *Grenadier*. For the rest of the war the area was patrolled by the British and Dutch submarines, which became more and more numerous as time went by.

Sadly, British operations in Burma in 1943 did not reach a state whereby they became the expected major offensive to liberate the country. This only became possible the following year, by which time there were enough British submarines available to intercept the limited amount of Japanese shipping between Singapore and Burma.

The only patrol by an American submarine off the west coast of Malaya and Thailand had ended with its loss. It seems that for political motives the *Grenadier* was sent to this area where there were few targets. She was caught unexpectedly on the surface and attacked by a Japanese aircraft that proved wounding. The boat subsequently had to be scuttled despite many hours of strenuous efforts to make her seaworthy again. It was a classic case of political expediency over-ruling military prudence.

Notes:

1 S.E. Morison: *History of US Naval Operations in WW2, Volume IV,* page 188.

2 *ibid.*

3 Commander Submarine Force, COMSUBFORCE, *Current Doctrine Submarines*, 1939.

4 Morison credits Lieutenant Commander F. Warder of the *Seawolf* with two hits; Alden with more recent information gives only one hit.

5 Nimitz later commanded the USS *Haddo* (SS-255).

6 *One of Our Submarines* by Edward Young published by Rupert Hart-Davis.

7 Commander Submarine Force, Pacific Fleet, serial 00349 dated 21 September 1945: POW Statements covering loss of US Submarines, Statement by Lieutenant Commander J.A. Fitzgerald, USN.

8 *The Pacific Campaign* by Dan van der Vat published by Hodder & Stoughton, 1992.

9 Signal timed 1435/2 March 1943 from cominch to Admiralty (classified HUSH MOST SECRET) quoted in letter to the author from the Naval Historical Branch (MOD). Also quoted in Maurice Matloff's *Strategic Planning for Coalition Warfare 1943-44.*

10 British Naval Staff History, *Submarines Volume III, The Far East.*

11 *Strategic Planning for Coalition Warfare 1943-44*, by Maurice Matloff, US Army in World War II Series, Washington DC 1959.

12 *Silent Victory* by Clay Blair published by Doubleday 1966.

Seven
The British Return

On the outbreak of war with Germany in 1939 the Royal Navy had a submarine flotilla in the Far East, based in Hong Kong. The submarines were soon deployed to other more active theatres of war, and indeed by December 1941, when the war became truly a 'world war', seven of the original fifteen boats of this flotilla had already been sunk. By then there was only one British submarine in Eastern waters, the elderly HMS *Rover*, which was refitting in the dockyard at Singapore after being damaged by German bombers earlier that year in Crete.

As the Japanese Army advanced down the Malay peninsular the *Rover* was hastily made seaworthy and then towed to Batavia in Java. With the likelihood that the Dutch East Indies would also fall victim to Japanese aggression, the luckless submarine was towed first to Trincomalee and thence to Bombay where she completed her refit. However, despite the shortage of submarines she was never used operationally again.

During the morning of 10 December 1941 the new battleship HMS *Prince of Wales* and the battlecruiser *Repulse* had been sunk in the South China Sea by Japanese aircraft operating from the nominally Vichy-controlled French colony of Indo-China. Among the casualties was Admiral Sir Tom Phillips, who only days before had hoisted his flag as C-in-C of the Eastern Fleet. As soon as news of the disaster reached Singapore, Admiral Sir Geoffrey Layton resumed command of what was left of the fleet. One of his early requests to the Admiralty in London was for some submarines to be sent to the Far East as a matter of urgency.

The Mediterranean Fleet was also short of submarines; losses in the flotillas there had been heavy during 1941. Nevertheless, the *Trusty* (Lieutenant

Commander W.D.A. 'Bill' King) was sailed and arrived in Singapore on 31 January 1942. The *Truant* (Lieutenant Commander Hugh Haggard) followed, but had to be diverted to Surabaya, the Dutch naval base in Java, as Singapore had by then fallen to the Japanese. Both submarines were back in Colombo by early March, their crews exhausted. The tropical heat, the fact that the boats were crammed with additional crew and gear, the continual bombing when in harbour and the lack of success at sea had all taken their toll.

The submarines were available to carry out patrols in the Malacca Straits in anticipation of Vice Admiral Chuicho Nagumo's raid on, or perhaps invasion of, Ceylon that Easter. However, the Japanese Carrier Strike Force approached from the west of Sumatra and consequently the submarine patrol by the *Truant* failed to intercept. The *Truant* did manage to sink two Japanese transports but these were returning empty from the occupation of the Andaman Islands.

At the time of the Japanese strike on Ceylon, HMS *Trusty* was lying alongside the depot ship HMS *Lucia* preparing to embark torpedoes before going on patrol. Lieutenant Commander King was actually having breakfast when the alarm sounded. He recalls that as he reached the submarine's bridge he saw a stream of enemy aircraft burst out of a cloud off the harbour mouth and seemingly come straight at him. The submarine's signalman had manned a bren gun and was firing without success at the enemy as they flew low over the depot ship's masts. King could actually see the enemy pilots huddled in their cockpits. All the bombs dropped about twenty yards short except for one, which went through the deck of the *Lucia* and out again through the bottom of the ship without exploding. Some of the *Trusty*'s crew were in the depot ship at the time and were trapped by a watertight door which had become jammed; they had to squeeze out through a porthole and swim to the submarine.

Three weeks at sea was considered the most that could be achieved in the intolerable conditions of heat and humidity, and this permitted just one week in the patrol area. Only sporadic patrols could be carried out by the two British submarines and their Dutch colleagues. The arrival of HMS *Trident* in August did not improve the situation at all. She made one patrol, fired eight torpedoes at long range at a Japanese cruiser without success and then had to return with engine defects, which were in fact so serious that she had to leave for the UK for a refit.

This situation prevailed for the rest of 1942 and most of 1943, the limited Allied submarine effort being almost entirely in the hands of the Dutch. However, the Italian surrender in early September released a number of submarines from duty in the Mediterranean and by the end of October seven more boats[1] had arrived in Ceylon.

The conditions which these submarines encountered on patrol were very different from those they had experienced in the Mediterranean. No longer were they operating in clear seas; the waters of the Straits of Malacca were a dirty green

The ship's company of HMS Tally Ho. *(Ian Trenowden)*

colour with plenty of floating debris – branches from palm trees, coconuts, rotting vegetation and dead fish. The coast itself was low-lying, bordered with mangrove swamps and with few distinctive landmarks to aid navigation. Close inshore there were sandbanks, fishing strakes, strong tides and unpredictable currents, all adding to the submariners' worries.

The first of these submarines to go on patrol was the *Templar* (Lieutenant Commander D.J. Buckley), but poor weather and a defective radar made it an unproductive period and she was relieved by the *Tactician* (Lieutenant Commander A.F. Collett). Apart from carrying out a beach reconnaissance, her patrol too was uneventful. The pattern changed when HMS *Tally Ho* (Lieutenant Commander L.W.A. 'Ben' Bennington) sailed for the Penang area on 26 October.

One incident followed another almost from the moment the *Tally Ho* sailed from Colombo. On the first evening the Officer of the Watch sighted what he thought to be torpedo tracks approaching and the submarine dived rapidly. Two further false alarms occurred before they reached their patrol area. In the early hours of 2 November, as they approached Penang, the Officer of the Watch was startled to see a vast array of lights ahead. As it turned out, the lights were merely those of small fishing vessels – many of them so small that they were just an open boat with one man aboard. Bennington turned away towards Sumatra so as not to prejudice his arrival in the area.

At dusk on the evening of 6 November 1943, while Bennington was stalking a small freighter, a German U-boat was seen leaving harbour[2] at Penang, an island off the west coast of Malaya north of the Malacca Strait. This was something that no one expected to see in the Far East at that time, but the silhouette was unmistakable. Seven minutes after the sighting Bennington fired five torpedoes at a range of just over a mile. To his amazement there was not a single hit. Worse, one torpedo was reported to have run wild and was coming back towards the *Tally Ho*. The crew listened with bated breath as it passed close up the port side. As for the U-boat, she remained on the surface and disappeared into the gloom.

On the 8th the *Tally Ho* again suffered from defective torpedoes when two were fired at a merchant ship leaving Penang. Both missed and again Bennington and his crew suffered the agonies of hearing one of their own torpedoes coming back towards them. Two days later they had their first success when five torpedoes were fired at a merchant ship, later identified as the *Kisogawa Maru*. Two minutes later a large explosion blew the enemy vessel apart, while a fire burning on the surface for some hours afterwards indicated that the target had been carrying petrol. However, once again there was a rogue torpedo which turned back towards them.

Early on the 12th another U-boat was sighted. Bennington's attack was foiled by the alertness of the escort, a Japanese destroyer, which sighted the *Tally Ho* and forced Bennington to dive. Only a half-hearted attack was made by the destroyer, which dropped four charges ineffectually before returning to the U-boat. Yet another U-boat was sighted that afternoon but no attack was possible as the U-boat innocently altered its course away.[3] That night the *Tally Ho* started the long passage back to Colombo. It had been a patrol full of incident and one that deserved better luck than to have attacks spoiled by defective torpedoes on three occasions.

On the morning of 14 November two submarines were approaching Penang, each unaware of the other's presence. One was HMS *Taurus* (Lieutenant Commander Mervyn Wingfield RN), at the end of a passage of nearly 1,300 miles from the base in Ceylon to her patrol area. The other, a Japanese boat, was at the beginning of what was planned to be a far longer voyage. The account of what followed is given by one of the British submarine's officers, Lieutenant John Gibson RNVR.[4]

The sea was like the surface of a mirror in a moonlit room. Rain squalls came down from the north, passing across the sea in noisy gusts, soaking the men on the bridge and chilling them. Visibility was poor.

The Taurus came on slowly towards the dark shape of the island. The enemy blackout was complete. The scene was dead. We did not know that to the south of us a Japanese U-boat was coming up the Straits. She was coming up from Singapore to join the enemy flotilla in Penang. As we cruised slowly in the shallows this other boat was getting closer. Unseen, unheard, she was creaming confidently through the pale waters.

Two miles off the entrance the Taurus *dived. The early light was dangerous. It was at this time that the enemy might send out air patrols and they would see us, a dark blob on the flatness. They would see our wake in the brilliant green phosphorescence. A silent drifting patrol boat would hear our diesels as we neared them. So we dived early. In these waters there was an uncertainty; the war was waiting to blow up, and each side was on guard. There was a pulsating stillness and for months there had been complete quiet. Submarines had not been operating here for some time. The Japanese were waiting, tense, motionless. They hung on to their steaming jungles and listened for the first light footfall that would mean that the Allies were about to strike. In that nervous and apprehensive state they were liable to be dangerous. We went carefully.*

But the U-boat coming from the south was without care, She came chugging along and her crew would be shaving and getting ready to go ashore. They would be looking forward to a hot breakfast. How well we knew that tendency to relax during the last few miles when home is in sight! That relaxation cost that crew their lives.

We were heading north, parallel to the coast, waiting for the sun to rise. Through the periscope the view was dim and rain squalls limited vision. The reflection of small black clouds swept across the moonlit surface. In the warm, well-lit messes we were having breakfast. The Officer of the Watch plotted our course on the chart and had another look at the long black island that lay against the sunrise. With routine thoroughness he swung round to look out to sea, his head covered in a black hood that hid the instrument lights from his eyes. He was able to adapt his sight to the deep blue light of morning seen through a periscope.

At 5.30 the enemy must have been about four miles away. He was eventually sighted at a range of two thousand yards [one nautical mile]. *By this time the sky was very much lighter, but the sun had not yet risen. It was an indistinct shape that was first seen, a black blob that came on through the rain squalls until it was suddenly in a clear patch. Then it was obvious – a U-boat! The most satisfactory of all targets. The news was through the boat in a flash. Perhaps it was the* I-8 – *a Japanese U-boat that had sunk a British vessel some months earlier and had then massacred the crew. Wingfield, by now at the periscope, was tense. We swung to port, and for an eternity the target was lost in a squall. Then Wingfield gave the order to fire; it was a snap attack, no deliberating, no calculation. The whole thing was over in three minutes and the torpedoes were on their way. By now the enemy diesels were were clearly heard on the hydrophones, dim and feeble behind the strident noise of six torpedo engines. Two thousand yards at 45 knots.[5] The single explosion was dead on time. It was a deep and thunderous roar and for a moment the whole boat shook. The Captain raised the periscope and had a look. Nothing in sight. Not a thing. The noise of diesels had ceased. Three minutes after the explosion, six after the first sighting, we were back in*

HMS/m Taurus [T-class] *at Barrow in 1942, underway in harbour and securing for sea. (RN Submarine Museum)*

our messes finishing our breakfasts. When Wingfield did that attack he was feeling very ill. He had a temperature of 102°.

The submarine sunk by the *Taurus* was the Japanese *I-34*, a submarine of over 2,000 tons surface displacement, a speed of 23 knots and a range of 14,000 miles. Like many Japanese submarines of that time she was fitted with a small hangar and carried a seaplane. She had only been completed in August the previous year. More importantly, she had been loaded with a cargo of rubber, tin, tungsten and quinine which she had been due to deliver to the Germans.[6] She sank in only 10 fathoms of water and in 1961 work began on salvaging the cargo.

After this successful start to the patrol the *Taurus* moved further south. The following morning, with the submarine on the surface, several patrol vessels were evaded. One, more skilful and tenacious than the rest, maintained contact with the submarine, which was moving at full speed on the diesels. By 4.00 a.m. the Japanese ship had closed to three miles and Wingfield decided to dive. Density layers caused trouble with the trim, not helped by the fact that neither ballast pump could obtain a suction. The submarine bottomed at 150 feet just as the Japanese vessel gained contact; it dropped two depth charges which caused only minor damage.

At six o'clock Wingfield decided that the longer he stayed where he was, the more opportunity the Japanese had to call for reinforcements. After placing all the submarine's confidential books in a weighted bag, which could easily be thrown overboard if necessary, and closing up the guns' crews, Wingfield attempted to come off the bottom and surface. The Japanese heard the submarine almost at once and came in to attack, dropping a pattern of seven depth charges. The force of the explosions lifted the submarine from the sea bed, barely under control. Again Lieutenant Gibson describes the scene dramatically:

Then the charges begin to explode. They come in towards us, a string of seven. The first is a noise that shakes us, and in that split second the last two charges come down almost on their mark. We do not hear their explosion, only that great crash as if a huge hammer had struck our thin plates. The lights flash and we are for a second in darkness. Then the fun really starts and things begin to go wrong. We slip at an angle in some direction or other. God knows where. The compass bell, the alarm, rings stridently to tell us we have no gyro. The steering and hydroplane wheels spin loosely. They are dead in the hands that frantically try to guide us. All the depth gauges are out; one says four hundred feet and the other, twenty. Somewhere in the maze of telemotor pipes there is a deafening scream where the whole system is on strike. From forward we hear that long steady hiss that is our valuable compressed air escaping into the boat. In the darkness we stumble around and find the leaks and faults; but that damned noise goes on.

In the engine room they have a depth-gauge that seems fairly reasonable, and we form a chain of men to pass the information to the control room. In a matter of seconds the emergency lighting comes on and at last we can raise the periscopes. Meanwhile, we are still at a sharp angle and the deck is slippery. The engineers patter around in silence with their torches and spanners. 'Up periscope!'

As the captain puts his eye to the lens his voice is sharp. 'We are on the surface. Gun action. Blow main ballast. Enemy bearing red four five.' The hatches open as the gun crew tumble up to the gun. For a moment the sunlight blinds us – then we see the chaser over to port; we can hear his machine guns chattering and his gun flashes out a warning. The shot falls harmlessly over our heads.

A hot engagement then took place. The Japanese ship received several hits, one of which put her gun out of action. Further hits were secured on the steering, bridge and engine room. Before the *Taurus* could finish off her opponent an aircraft appeared and came in to the attack. Wingfield decided that it was time to dive and pressed the klaxon. During the thirteen minutes that they had been on the surface all defects had been made good and the submarine was once again fully under control. She made off to seaward at sixty feet, leaving the Japanese behind.

It had been an exciting two days for the submarine's crew. The remainder of the patrol was less so, though it was not entirely without incident. The *Taurus* moved area twice in an attempt to find a suitable target. Only one ship was sighted, a large escorted merchant ship on passage to Rangoon, but she was too far away for the submarine to get within range. There were many junks to be seen but at that stage of the war they were left alone. This later changed when they were taken over by the Japanese to carry supplies for their army and so became legitimate targets, to be sunk by gunfire as they were too small for torpedoes to hit.

Returning to Colombo, the need for efficient lookout was demonstrated when they were only 250 miles out and were attacked by a Japanese seaplane, which came in from astern. The bombs exploded harmlessly in the wake as the submarine dived to safety.

By the end of 1943 the submarines had become firmly established in Ceylon. They had HMS *Adamant* as their depot ship, and with its arrival the 4th Flotilla, as it was known, moved from Colombo to Trincomalee. Throughout 1944 the flotilla was steadily reinforced as more and more submarines became available. In March a second depot ship, HMS *Maidstone*, arrived and the force was split into two flotillas, the 4th and the 8th. Later still a third depot ship, HMS *Wolfe*, arrived from the UK and the *Maidstone* took her flotilla down to Fremantle to join the American South West Pacific command.

New construction submarines arriving in the Far East were all fitted with air-conditioning units, which to some extent helped to make life onboard more bearable. They also had some ballast tanks converted to carry oil fuel, giving them greater range. For the *Tally Ho*, one of the early arrivals on station, numbers 3 and 5 main ballast tanks had been modified in Port Said within a few days on a self-help basis, allowing for about an extra 100 tons of fuel to be carried, thereby increasing the range by over a thousand miles.[7] The work was carried out by the boat's Engineer Officer, Lieutenant Peter Scott-Maxwell RNVR, but such unofficial alterations and additions did not meet with Admiralty approval. Eventually they agreed that the extra fuel could be used on passage to the patrol billet but any remaining had to be flushed out on arrival.[8] It was hardly a sensible compromise since the fuel flushed from the tanks would remain on the surface, betraying the fact that a submarine had recently been in the area.

Another boat, the *Tantalus*, had a very different experience. Her construction had been completed at Barrow in mid-May 1943, and there had been talk of the ship builders carrying out this modification to the ballast tanks, where it was expected that the work could be finished with little effect on the boat's completion. But it was not to be; the Admiralty ordered the work to be done later in Portsmouth Dockyard. So, after trials, the work-up, and an initial patrol inside the Arctic Circle near Bear Island, the submarine found herself in the dockyard. It was three months before the work was complete[9] and the *Tantalus* ready to continue to the Far East.

Lieutenant Commander Bennington, the Commanding Officer of HMS Tally Ho, *at the periscope. (Ian Trenowden)*

The *Tally Ho* continued her successes of late 1943 into the new year. She was off Penang on 9 January 1944 when the 5,500 ton Japanese cruiser *Kuma* was sighted. To the chagrin of the entire crew, the cruiser zigzagged away before Bennington could make an attack. It was therefore all the more gratifying when the same ship was sighted again two days later. A bow salvo of seven torpedoes – one was unserviceable – was fired at a range of just under a mile. This time there were no rogues. Two large explosions were heard in rapid succession, and these hits were sufficient to sink the cruiser. The escorting Japanese destroyer reacted quickly and the *Tally Ho* was subjected to a number of counter-attacks. Eighteen depth charges were dropped, of which only the first two were considered to be 'close'. The submarine crept away from the scene, heading inshore where she was least expected to go. Before the patrol was over another attack was made, which resulted in the sinking of a merchant ship, the *Ryuko Maru*, off the Nicobar islands on 14 January. Bennington fired six torpedoes from the surface in bright moonlight at his target and had the satisfaction of seeing her sink to the bottom.

The *Tally Ho*'s first three patrols had proved remarkable in their success and in the high number of incidents. She sailed from Trincomalee on 3 February for her fourth patrol. Bennington planned to work his way south of the One Fathom

Bank in the Malacca Straits, hoping to find plenty of traffic to attack. However, Japanese patrols in the area made this difficult, so he abandoned the idea as he had a Special Operation to carry out later[10] which could not be compromised by his detection at this stage. On the night of 14/15 February the submarine retired to a position in the middle of the Strait to recharge its batteries. After this essential operation had been completed Bennington decided to move in towards the coast. At 5.15 a.m., while proceeding on the surface, the Officer of the Watch sighted what he thought was a surfaced U-boat. Bennington was already on the bridge at the time of the sighting and immediately took over. The U-boat was almost dead ahead and proceeding northwards at about 14 knots. Bennington could at least be certain that the target was an enemy since no other British or Dutch boats were in the area. A snap attack was called for.

As Bennington began to alter course to bring the *Tally Ho* into an attacking position, the other submarine was lost in an isolated patch of mist. Then, just as the submarine was steadying up on a firing course which would give the torpedoes a track angle of 120° and a running range of under two miles, the report was made: 'Second U-boat broad on the port bow'. Bennington acknowledged the report and gave the order to fire at the first target before issuing the instruction to dive. As Bennington went below it was reported that the second submarine was in fact only a junk.

As the *Tally Ho* went down to 80 feet the crew waited anxiously for some evidence of their success. At the expected time they were rewarded with the sound of a hit and the noise of the target's diesel engines ceased immediately. Bennington thought that the submarine was Japanese but it was in fact the German *UIT-23*, originally the Italian *Reginaldo Giuliani*, on her way from Singapore to Penang and thence to France with a cargo of tin which was desperately required to support the Third Reich's war machine. Although the *UIT-23* (*Kapitänleutnant* Werner Streigler) was hit just forward of the conning tower, there were a number of survivors,[11] who were picked up by an Arado float-plane which had been sent out to look for the U-boat when she failed to arrive at Penang. Frighteningly, they were lashed to the aircraft's floats for the twenty mile flight to shore.

On 24 February the *Tally Ho* was patrolling off the Sembilan Islands, where two days previously a Japanese merchant ship had been sunk by a single hit from their salvo of five torpedoes. That evening Bennington decided to proceed southwards on the surface towards the One Fathom Bank. Towards midnight one of the lookouts sighted two wakes ahead, but it was too dark for the silhouette of a ship to be seen. To Bennington, who had been called to the bridge, the bow wake had the appearance of an approaching surfaced submarine and he was uncertain whether it was enemy or friendly. He had to be sure, as both the *Truculent* and the *Tactician* were known to be in adjacent areas. The immediate need was to avoid a

The Tally Ho *in dry dock, showing the damage caused to the port ballast tanks by the*

propeller of a Japanese destroyer. (Ian Trenowden)

collision and Bennington altered course sharply to port and increased speed to full as the other vessel slid across the submarine's stern.

A signalled challenge from the *Tally Ho* brought no reply. Instead the other vessel bore down on the submarine at full speed, dropping depth charges. Only rapid alterations of course by Bennington avoided a violent impact. The enemy ship was faster and better armed than the submarine, and if the *Tally Ho* dived she would present a perfect target for ramming, gunfire and depth charges while she was seeking any safety in the depths. Bennington knew that his only chance was to keep end on to the enemy, altering course as late as possible when necessary to avoid ramming.

During one such manoeuvre the Japanese ship came in again, attempting to ram. Her funnel was clearly visible, belching smoke and sparks as her engine room crew gave full power, her bow wave creaming and foaming. At the last moment Bennington ordered: 'Hard a starboard.' It seemed at first that the submarine would surely be struck, but then she slowly began to turn and the vessels passed close to one another on opposing parallel courses. The submarine's Oerlikon gun had jammed, rendering the gunner unable to rake the enemy's bridge. The Japanese guns could not depress far enough to hit the submarine. The submariners' nostrils were assailed by the acrid stench of funnel gases and scorched paintwork as the other ship rushed by. One seaman remarked afterwards: 'If anyone had thrown so much as a potato he'd have got a VC.'

The Japanese ship was so close that the propeller on the starboard side tore at the *Tally Ho*. The rapidly revolving screw, made of hard phosphor bronze, bit into the mild steel of the port ballast tanks, ripping out chunks in a regular pattern as the ship passed down the submarine's side. Remarkably, the Japanese ship faded into the night and was not seen again. The submarine was damaged, but just how badly could not be assessed until daylight; in the meantime she was manoeuvrable, although listing badly. Bennington dived to await a chance to surface to look at the damage. While they waited there were some leaks to be attended to and other minor repairs to be carried out.

When the *Tally Ho* surfaced it was with little or no buoyancy on the port side and a 15° list, which was reduced to 12° by judicious flooding of internal tanks on the starboard side. In that manner, and with the ever-present threat that the submarine might make an involuntary dive, Bennington headed back to Trincomalee. Moving torpedoes around from the bow tubes to the starboard reload racks helped reduce the list still further. With the monsoon weather causing the submarine to roll considerably, the whole crew were greatly relieved to return to harbour. It required two months in dock to make the *Tally Ho* seaworthy again.

Another success in early 1944 occurred when the *Templar* (Lieutenant D.J. Beckley) damaged the cruiser *Kitagami*, which was escorted by three destroyers, in a night attack in the Malacca Strait. Beckley hit with two torpedoes from a salvo of eight fired at long range. It was the last attack by British submarines on Japanese heavy units until shortly before the end of the war. Even so, the boats were continually on patrol off the Malayan coast, attacking whatever shipping could be found and continuing the task of landing or recovering Special Forces, which had been performed to such great effect by the Dutch in 1942 and early 1943. U-boats, both Japanese and German, were seen from time to time, but attacks were unsuccessful until the *I-166* was sunk in July 1944.[12]

During this time one British submarine was lost, one of only three in this theatre of war. The *Stonehenge* sailed from Trincomalee on 25 February 1944 for patrol off the north coast of Sumatra and was never heard of again. The Japanese themselves did not claim this victory and the cause of her loss remains a mystery.

Notes:

1 HM Submarines *Severn, Templar, Tresspasser, Tally Ho, Tactician, Taurus* and *Surf.*

2 It is unclear from surviving German records which U-boat this was, or whether it was in fact arriving or departing. In any case, the Germans were unaware of the attack.

3 Again it has not been possible to identify the U-boats. One of them may have been the *U-183* which had arrived at Penang on 30 October and sailed for repairs in Singapore in early November.

4 *Dark Seas Above* by John Gibson (William Blackwood 1947).

5 Gibson's timings and attack details do not always match the official figures given in Wingfield's Patrol Report, but this in no way detracts from his account of events.

6 *The Penang Submarines* by Dennis Gunton published by Phoenix Press in Penang. After salvage the submarine's bell was given to the Mariner's Club in Penang.

7 *The T Class Submarine* by Paul Kemp, Arms & Armour Press, 1990

8 *The Hunting Submarine* by Ian Trenowden, William Kimber 1974.

9 *The Sword of Damocles* by Admiral Sir Hugh Mackenzie (Submarine Museum 1994).

10 This was Operation GUSTAVUS VI, the last of clandestine operations previously carried out by the Dutch submarines (see Chapter Four). On this occasion the *Tally Ho* was required to embark two officers and eight other ranks, with all their stores, and then land them in Japanese occupied Malaya.

11 *Wings of the Dawning* by Arthur Banks (Images Publishing 1996) gives the number of survivors as fifteen.

12 See Chapter Nine.

Eight
The Germans and Italians

Operations by the German U-boats during the Second World War are inevitably linked with the name of Karl Dönitz. During the First World War he saw action in the cruiser *Breslau* before being posted to U-boats, and served during 1917 under the 'ace' *Kapitänleutnant* Walter Forstmann. In 1918 he commanded the *UB-68* in the Mediterranean; he was captured in October when the submarine was sunk while attacking a convoy. When the U-boat arm was revived in 1935 Dönitz became *Führer der U-Boote*. In October 1939 he was promoted Rear Admiral and became *Befehlshaber der U-Boote* (BdU). Early in 1943 Grand Admiral Raeder resigned as Commander-in-Chief of the Navy and on 30 January Dönitz was promoted to succeed him. However, he remained BdU and moved the U-boat Headquarters to Berlin so that he could retain personal control of operations.

Dönitz was convinced that the Battle of the Atlantic was vital for German victory in the war. He constantly refused to divert U-boats to areas which he considered to be of little value in winning the battle. Only when the longer range U-boats became available and losses in the Atlantic became unacceptably high would Dönitz countenance operations in the Indian Ocean.

The idea of German submarines operating in the Far East was first considered as early as November 1939. In a report made to the Führer on 10 November by Admiral Raeder,[1] the Commander-in-Chief suggested that Japan be asked to cede several submarines to Germany for warfare against the British in the Far East, as the German U-boats then in commission did not even have the range to operate as far afield as the Cape of Good Hope. At a similar meeting with the Führer on 22 November it was stated that it was expected that the Japanese would agree to this proposal. Despite this optimism, the minutes of a third meeting, on 8 December, laconically record that the Japanese had replied 'that no submarines will be available.' The views of Dönitz on this proposed dilution of his trained crews are not recorded.

In the middle of December 1941, just ten days after the extension of the war to the Far East, Admiral Fricke, Chief of Staff *Oberkommando der Kriegsmarine* (OKM), the German equivalent of the British Admiralty, met with Vice Admiral Naokuni Nomura, the Japanese Naval Attaché in Berlin, to discuss the delimitation of the respective operational areas of the German and Japanese Navies. The Japanese proposed that the boundary should be longitude 70° East, but the Germans desired a diagonal across the Indian Ocean from the Gulf of Aden to Northern Australia. They suspected that Japanese insistence on the 70° line was connected with their territorial ambitions in Asia – the line of longitude ran southwards from a point which would leave both east and west coasts of India in the Japanese controlled area, except for the port of Karachi. In the end, an agreement between Germany, Italy and Japan on 18 January 1942 accepted the 70° line, with the proviso that 'in the Indian Ocean operations may be carried out beyond the agreed boundary if the situation requires.'

Survivors from a British ship, which had been sunk in the Atlantic by the Italian submarine Cappellini, *are given food and water before being directed towards the nearest land. (Ufficio Storico della Marina Militaire, Rome)*

By May 1942 the fortunes of the Axis Powers were at their peak. Germany and Japan never came nearer to joining hands. While adequate numbers of targets could be found in the North Atlantic, Dönitz did not send U-boats to the Cape of Good Hope or even further afield into the Indian Ocean. Because of the vast distances involved, such an undertaking would not have been profitable. However, by the end of 1942 'the happy time' off America's east coast was over and Allied anti-submarine measures were making patrols in the mid-Atlantic increasingly hazardous for the U-boats. Consequently the larger Type IXC U-boats were sent first to patrol off Freetown, then progressively off the Congo and the Cape itself. The Type IX U-boat – in seven successive variants – was intended for distant operations, possessing good sea-keeping qualities and long range. The earlier boats had a range of 8,100 miles at 12 knots, though they had a maximum speed of just over 18 knots, while in the later boats of the Type XID$_2$ variant the range had been increased to 23,700 miles.[2]

The first four boats to be sent to the Cape were known as *Gruppe Eisbär* ('Polar Bear'): *U-68, U-156, U-172* and *U-504*, all Type IXC. While still on passage on 12 September 1942 the *U-156*, commanded by *Korvettenkapitän* Werner Hartenstein, sank the British liner *Laconia* and then found that it had been carrying 1,800 Italian POWs and their Polish guards together with some British families returning home from Kenya, a total of over 2,700 people including the crew. A rescue operation was organised by Hartenstein, who was joined by other submarines operating in the South Atlantic, including the Italian *Commandante Alfredo Cappellini* (*Capitano di Corvetta* Marco Revedin), but a submarine is a poor place to try and cope with hundreds of survivors. The rescue was not helped by an American aircraft bombing the *U-156* as it towed four lifeboats and displayed a large red cross.[3] As a result, Hartenstein had to stop towing the lifeboats and was forced to place all the survivors who had been onboard the submarine into the already crowded boats. Most survivors were eventually picked up by the French cruiser *Gloire* and two sloops from Dakar. Although the incident took place in the Atlantic, it is mentioned here not only because it illustrates the problems facing the U-boat commanders so far from their bases but also because it led to Admiral Dönitz issuing his order to all U-boats not to pick up survivors in the future – an order for which he was subsequently indicted at Nuremburg.

The *U-156* had been damaged by the American bombing; both periscopes were not fully functional, there was some minor flooding, but more importantly seven battery cells were cracked. The submarine was forced to return to France, its place in the group was taken by the *U-159* (*Kapitänleutnant* Helmut Witte), which had been patrolling off the Congo.

Opening their attack in the area to the south of Capetown, the group initially sank thirteen ships in three days before heavy storms and bad visibility resulted in the submarines being unable to find further quarry; two boats began the long return passage without expending all their torpedoes. The *U-504* (*Korvettenkapitän* Fritz Poske) and *U-159* went eastwards as far as Durban, where they met with some further success before they too returned to France. The deployment of *Gruppe Eisbär* was one of the most successful U-boat operations of the war; the four boats sank a total of twenty-three ships off South Africa with another eleven while on passage to and from the area. To this total must be added the three ships sunk by Hartenstein's *U-156* which had been unable to complete the mission.

An additional four submarines – *U-177, U-178, U-179* and *U-181* – arrived off the South African coast in the latter half of October. These were Type IXD$_2$ boats with the greater length and displacement and increased range over the earlier Type IXC boats. The force was not named as a formal *Gruppe* and was ordered to round the Cape of Good Hope and operate eastwards into the Indian Ocean to maintain the pressure on the limited Allied anti-submarine resources in the area.

The first to arrive was the *U-179* (*Korvettenkapitän* Ernst Sobe) and he immediately sank the British cargo ship *City of Athens* eighty miles south of Capetown. That evening HMS *Active*, which had sped to the area to pick up survivors, detected the submarine on the surface by radar and made a depth charge attack as the U-boat dived. The explosions briefly blew the *U-179* back to the surface before she disappeared from sight to be lost with all hands.

The waters off the southern coast of South Africa are notorious for the foul weather to be found there. When *Fregattenkapitän* Hans Ibbeken began operations in the *U-178* south of Cape Agulhas he quickly learned of the problems facing a submariner attacking in these waters and found them not unlike those in mid-Atlantic. On 26 October he sighted a ship of about 8,000 to 10,000 tons on the port bow and dived to attack. His log records: 'It is very difficult to hold the boat level when submerged. In spite of full speed I am unable to approach closer than 1,500 metres.' After firing two torpedoes without success he abandoned the chase. The following day a large tanker was sighted but although the *U-178* gave chase for most of the day Ibbeken was unable to make an attack before the target was lost in a rain squall as darkness closed in. Once again the U-boat's log records her Captain's frustration: 'I did not fire as the rough sea would make the straight run of a torpedo very doubtful. When will the weather improve?' The *U-178* headed for calmer waters off Durban.

One of the victims of the *U-177* (*Korvettenkapitän* Robert Gysae) was the steamer *Nova Scotia*, sunk on 28 November 1942 after being hit by 3 torpedoes. Apart from her crew and over 100 South African soldiers, the ship was carrying 756 Italian civilians from Massawa to Durban for internment. As the *Nova Scotia* sank she was burning furiously amidships and when the submarine surfaced Gysae found there were hundreds of survivors in the sea, most of them Italian, with all too few lifeboats. Two Italian merchant sailors who had become separated from the rest of the survivors were taken onboard the submarine before Gysae reluctantly left the area 'because of danger from air attack and the vicinity of the coast.'

The situation was similar to that prevailing at the time of the sinking of the *Laconia* only two months earlier. Gysae reported the sinking to U-boat headquarters and received the reply:[4] 'Continue operating. Waging war comes first. No rescue attempts.' However, the Germans did inform the Portuguese and the sloop *Alfonso de Albuquerque* was sent from Lourenco Marques to pick up the survivors. Eventually just 182 were rescued from the water.

Two days later Gysae hit the *Llandaff Castle* with two torpedoes. After the crew abandoned ship the submarine surfaced and approached the survivors with her deck guns manned. Speaking in good English, Gysae hailed the boats and enquired if anyone needed medical attention and whether they had sufficient provisions in the lifeboats. He gave them a course to steer for the nearest land and wished them a safe return to their families before proceeding to finish off the badly listing ship with gunfire.[5]

The *U-181* was commanded by the legendary *Kapitänleutnant* Wolfgang Lüth, destined to receive the highest decorations awarded by Germany. After seven

Wolfgang Lüth.

weeks at sea Lüth brought his submarine to a position just south of Capetown, 7,500 miles from Kiel. It is to the credit of the German submariners that, after this amount of time at sea, most war patrols would have been over and the crews would be relaxing back in their base, but for the *U-181*, and indeed for other U-boats sent to the Indian Ocean, the patrol was only just beginning. Over the following weeks the *U-181* was to range along the coast of South Africa and then northwards towards the Mozambique Channel. One of Lüth's early victims was the Panamanian registered steamship *Plaudit*. In heavy seas Lüth's first torpedo attack was unsuccessful. In worsening weather the submarine sought all day to regain a firing position while the crew strove to reload the torpedoes. That evening the *Plaudit* was hit, but did not sink. Lüth ordered the ship to be sunk by gunfire. With the gun's crew ever liable to be swept overboard as the waves broke over the submarine's casing, they secured eight hits on the ship before she sank.

At the end of November, off Lourenco Marques, the Greek steamer *Cleanthis* was missed with two torpedoes. Despite the fact that the Greek ship was armed Lüth decided to finish her off with his gun, but from a safe range of 3,000 yards. It was a risky decision; one hit from the merchant ship's gun would have had dangerous consequences for a submarine so far from its base. After the first round from the submarine the steamer's crew abandoned ship and headed for the shore. Eventually, having fired eighty rounds of 105mm shells, the Greek ship sank beneath the waves; the submarine's ammunition had been exhausted. It was not only British commanding officers who expended large quantities of gun ammunition![6]

Only once during the *U-181*'s patrol were the crew to suffer the anxiety of being depth charged. Off Durban in mid-November the destroyer HMS *Inconstant* spent a whole day hunting an elusive asdic contact, dropping patterns of depth charges whenever there was an opportunity. In late afternoon the destroyer was joined by two corvettes – HMS *Jasmine* and *Nigella*. When the destroyer had to return to Durban the two smaller ships continued carrying out sporadic attacks until after dark, when they too left for Durban. Lüth waited until midnight before bringing the *U-181* to the surface. The damage to the submarine was soon repaired.

During the patrol Lüth himself received information that he had been awarded the Oak Leaves to his Knight's Cross of the Iron Cross. In November 1942 he was the most successful U-boat commander still at sea. In terms of total tonnage sunk he was second only to Otto Kretschmer, who was then in a POW camp in Canada. Lüth's patrol in the *U-181* was to last until 18 January 1943, when the boat entered one of the huge concrete pens that had been built at Bordeaux. The submarine's log summed up the patrol succinctly:

> *Boat was at sea for a total of 129 days and sailed 21,369 miles. Twelve ships were sunk in the Capetown-Lourenco Marques area for a total of 57,000 GRT.*[7]

12.U-Flottille
Bordeaux

Above left: *Fregattenkapitän Klaus Scholtz.* Above right: *Badge of the 12th U-boat flotilla based at Bordeaux. This flotilla consisted of many of the German submarines which operated in the Indian Ocean.*

The Italian submarine *Ammiraglio Cagni* was one of a class of four submarines which at that time were the largest built in Italy and which had been completed in mid-1941. They had a fuel capacity of 180 tons giving them a range of over 10,000 miles at 12 knots. Although designed with a powerful torpedo armament of 14 tubes for attacking ocean shipping, these submarines were largely wasted in the Mediterranean on supply runs between Italy and North Africa, where three of the class were lost. In the autumn of 1942 the *Cagni* (*Capitano di Fregata* Carlo Liannaza) sailed from La Maddalena on 6 October with instructions to patrol off the Cape Town approaches and off South West Africa. She passed safely through the Straits of Gibraltar and had her first success while still north of Ascension Island. On 29 November she was 55 miles south-west of Cape Town and sank the Greek steamer *Argo*. She met with no further success and began her return voyage. On 13 January 1943 she met with the *U-459*, a special U-tanker,[8] or *Milch Kuh* as such a boat was known, which was accompanying the *Gruppe Seehund* ('Seal'). The submarine went on to patrol off St Paul's Rock off the South American coast before reaching Bordeaux on 20 February. It was a record for an Italian submarine of 137 days at sea, with 12,000 miles steamed for just two ships sunk.

After the fall of France in 1940 bases on the west coast of France became available for U-boats operating in the Atlantic. One of these bases was Bordeaux, which had the disadvantage of being some sixty miles from the sea up the Gironde river but the advantage that it was furthest away from the bases of any British aircraft. It was in Bordeaux that the *12 U-Flotille* was formed under the command of *Korvettenkapitän* Klaus Scholtz which eventually consisted of U-boats operating in the South Atlantic and the Indian Ocean. Scholtz, later promoted to *Fregattenkapitän*, was well qualified for the post having won the *Ritterkreuz* and subsequently the Oak Leaves while in command of the Type IXB *U-108*. The Italian submarines under the command of *Amiraglio* Angelo Parona shared the base with their German allies.

The U-boat base at Bordeaux was built on the northern edge of the town alongside one of the two non-tidal Basins and consisted of eleven pens providing fifteen sheltered berths for submarines, three of them being dry docks. The scale of the construction may be judged by the fact that the bomb-proof roof was almost 20 feet thick. Other concrete bunkers provided safe storage for ammunition, stores and fuel. Entrance to the Basin from the Gironde was through two parallel locks, the most vulnerable part of system. Construction began in 1943 to build a third lock which would be protected from air attack but the work was never finished.

The five boats of *Gruppe Seehund* left their French base early in 1943 and returned to Lorient in early May. Apart from *Kapitänleutnant* Georg Lassan in the *U-160*, who had claimed sinking ten ships but actually sank only seven and damaged two others, results had been disappointing. The whole group accounted for only twenty ships sunk and damage to two others, about half the success achieved by *Gruppe Eisbär*. Greater awareness by the British in South Africa of the U-boat threat and the introduction of convoys for some of the shipping were certainly one reason for the poor results of the *Gruppe Seehund*.

As the submarines of *Gruppe Seehund* withdrew from the area, the new Italian submarine *Leonardo da Vinci*[9] (*Capitano di Corvetta* Gianfranco Gazzana) arrived on station. While on passage Gazzana torpedoed the large troopship *Empress of Canada*, and then sank a further five ships during his patrol. One of Gazzana's victims was the British merchant ship *Manaar*, the Master being taken onboard the submarine for return to Germany, leaving a badly injured lascar seaman, the sole survivor from a previous sinking, in exchange. On 23 May the *Leonardo da Vinci* herself was sunk by two British escorts as she was about to enter the Bay of Biscay after ninety-three days at sea. There were no survivors.

Meanwhile the German boats continued to operate south of Capetown and eastwards towards Durban and into the Indian Ocean. The heavy losses incurred by the U-boats in the North Atlantic in early 1943 convinced Admiral Dönitz that

133

it would be more profitable, and less costly, to operate in areas such as this. By June there were six U-boats on patrol in the Indian Ocean, including Lüth's *U-181*, which had sailed from Bordeaux on 24 March for this second patrol. Towards the end of June all of these U-boats were fuelled by the tanker *Charlotte Schliemann* in an area about 600 miles south of Mauritius – an area remote from the usual shipping lanes and one unlikely to be patrolled by any aircraft.

The *U-181* had been fuelled and provisioned for eighteen weeks before sailing, and her crew looked forward to their return to Bordeaux by 1 August. Halfway into his patrol Lüth received a signal instructing all the Type IXD$_2$ boats in the Indian Ocean to rendezvous with a tanker which would give them additional fuel and supplies to enable them to remain at sea for twenty-six weeks. The *U-181* sighted the tanker on 22 June and the crew were surprised to see that the *U-178* and *U-196* were already alongside fuelling and that there were two other U-boats waiting their turn. When the *U-181* eventually went alongside to fuel many of the crew took advantage of the occasion to shower and stretch their legs onboard the tanker. Lüth recorded in his log his dissatisfaction with the amount of meat and vegetables with which they had been supplied, feeling that they were unlikely to last for the extended length of the patrol.

Another of Lüth's victims was the Swedish merchant ship *Sicilia*, which had been sighted leaving the port of Lourenco Marques. Her sinking was unusual as it was conducted in accordance with the long abandoned German version of the *Prize Regulations*. The ship was stopped by a shot across the bows and the Master

Focke-Achgelis Fa 330

Sketch of the Bachstelze *which was fitted to type IXD$_2$ U-boats to improve the range of visibility while operating in the Indian Ocean.*

ordered to board the submarine with the ship's papers. After finding that the ship's registration was not recorded, her papers were incomplete and she had made several earlier trips to and from Allied ports, Lüth decided to sink her. The crew were given thirty minutes to pack their bags and abandon ship before she was sunk by a single torpedo.

The basing of German U-boats in Penang for operations in the Indian Ocean was again proposed by the Japanese in December 1942, but this was not considered viable at that time until the necessary stocks of fuel, lubricating oil, ammunition, consumable stores, spare parts and suitable provisions were available. In the spring of 1943, when the matter was again raised by the Japanese, it was also suggested that two U-boats should be turned over to them in order that they might be copied. Dönitz saw no point in agreeing to this request since, in his opinion, the Japanese would be incapable of building these boats on a scale large enough to make an impact on the war against Allied shipping. However, Hitler had other views and it was decided that the Japanese should be given two U-boats in return for supplies of rubber. The *U-511* became Hitler's personal gift to Emperor Hirohito and left Germany in April 1943.[10]

With adequate targets to be found in the North Atlantic Dönitz was reluctant to divert resources to an area where the immense distances involved would make the patrols unprofitable. By early 1943 the U-boats were already operating off the Cape of Good Hope and even eastwards and northwards into the southern Indian Ocean, while in the North Atlantic it was becoming more and more difficult for the U-boats and they were suffering increasing losses. The time was propitious for another extension to the U-boats' operating areas.

Dönitz felt that the best results could be obtained by a surprise attack in the Northern Indian Ocean, which would be new ground for the Germans and where the Japanese had made few patrols. Such an attack could not be made until the end of September 1943, when the south-east monsoon would be over. It was planned that between six and nine U-boats would sail from Europe in June for this offensive.

Meanwhile the operations off the south-east coast of Africa had to continue. After their successful replenishment from the *Charlotte Schliemann* the *U-178* and the *U-196* were sent to the Mozambique Channel, while the *U-197* and *U-198* were further south between Lourenco Marques and Durban. Lüth – by then promoted to *Korvettenkapitän* and the holder of the Knight's Cross with Oak Leaves and Swords – took his *U-181* towards Mauritius, and the *U-177* was given an area south of Madagascar where Allied air activity was thought to be least. This was because Gysae's *U-177* was equipped with a small single seat helicopter, the Fa-330, known as the *Bachstelze*.

More correctly, the *Bachstelze* was a towed autogyro which became airborne as its three-bladed rotor was rotated by the wind and the forward speed of the submarine. The machine, tethered to the after end of the submarine's conning tower by 500 feet of cable, rose to a height of about 400 feet, giving the observer a greatly increased horizon of about 25 nautical miles compared to about 5 miles from the conning tower of the submarine. From his lofty perch the pilot could report any sightings by telephone to the submarine. Normally the aircraft would be winched down, dismantled and stowed in two watertight containers aft of the conning tower. It was a tricky task and took about twenty minutes to complete. In an emergency the tow line could be cut and the machine would descend slowly into the sea, allowing the submarine to dive quickly. With luck the pilot would be picked up when it was safe for the submarine to surface again, but it illustrates the need for the submarine to be operating in an area where air patrols were considered unlikely.

As a result of a sighting from the *U-177*'s *Bachstelze* the Greek steamer *Eithalia Mari* was attacked and sunk on 6 August 1943, the only time the use of this unusual machine resulted in a successful interception and attack. The British remained unaware of this new development for another nine months until the *U-852* (*Kapitänleutnant* Heinz-Wilhelm Eck) was driven ashore near the Horn of Africa in May 1944 and the remains of the damaged hull, with its stored aircraft, could be inspected.

Incidentally, in May 1944 the *U-181*, by then commanded by *Kapitän zur See* Kurt Freiwald, was flying its *Bachstelze* when the cable snapped as the submarine was heading into a strong wind. The machine spiralled awkwardly down into the sea, hitting the surface with a big splash. Before the submarine could turn and pick up the hapless pilot he was attacked by several seabirds who thought that the struggling man was a floundering fish. He was quickly brought aboard – severely pecked but otherwise safe – but the submarine's crew were not sorry to see the end of the machine.

Of the six U-boats which had been operating in the Indian Ocean, five began their return to France in August 1943; the sixth – the *U-178* (*Korvettenkapitän* Wilhelm Dommes) – went to Penang, where she berthed by the end of the month. It was at this time that the Germans suffered their next loss in this area when, south of Madagascar, the *U-197* (*Korvettenkapitän* Robert Bartels) was damaged in an attack by a Catalina aircraft. Bartels manoeuvred his U-boat brilliantly to thwart the aircraft's attacks while his gunners did their best to shoot it down. The first aircraft had to leave the scene with the U-boat listing badly, unable to dive but still capable of hitting back at its tormentors. More aircraft arrived at the scene and eventually Bartel's luck ran out. The U-boat disappeared in a flurry of oil and the foam of bursting depth charges. There were no survivors.

The full story of the loss of the *U-197* caused controversy among the other U-boat commanders in the area. Bartels had managed to signal the other U-boats

A Catalina *flying boat, which carried out most of the long-range anti-submarine patrols in the Indian Ocean. (Bob Honeywood)*

that he was under attack, a message which was received by the *U-181* and *U-196* when they were on the surface within sight of each other. Using semaphore flags there was an angry exchange of signals between *Korvettenkapitän* Eitel-Friedrich Kentrat in the *U-196* and Lüth, which is recorded in the log of the former. Kentrat wrote that he signalled Lüth that they should turn east and try to help Bartels. He added that Lüth's attitude was 'incomprehensible'. At first Lüth had turned east, but then said that he was short of fuel and must continue homeward. As the two submarines parted in opposite directions Kentrat continued to try and persuade Lüth to join him but to no avail. Kentrat spent two or three days looking for his ill-fated friend before he too turned for home.[11]

Both the *U-181* and *U-196* reached Bordeaux in mid-October 1943. Lüth had spent a record breaking $29\frac{1}{2}$ weeks at sea, a record which stood for only a few days until Kentrat arrived having been at sea for $31\frac{1}{2}$ weeks. These two patrols are testimony to the high morale of the two crews and to the outstanding leadership of the two commanding officers. Lüth wrote a short thesis[12] on the subject based on his own methods. In addition to the usual round of tournaments and quizzes he introduced the idea of giving 'leave onboard', whereby the man was excused all duties except action stations. The same qualities of leadership were necessary in other commanding officers whose boats were sent to the Indian Ocean but whose time at sea, though long, did not reach these record-breaking proportions.

A second patrol by the *Ammiraglio Cagni* under the command of *Capitano di Corvetta* G. Roselli-Lorenzini, had lasted eighty-four days when news was received of the Italian capitulation. Roselli-Lorenzini made for Durban, where the submarine was interned. During this patrol the *Cagni* had reported an attack against a carrier escorted by three destroyers, but in fact had badly damaged the armed merchant cruiser HMS *Asturias*.

The nine Type IXC U-boats of the *Monsun* group left their bases for the Indian Ocean in late June or early July 1943. It was planned that the Type XIV *Milch Kuh* *U-462* should accompany the group to refuel them off the coast of Brazil but the tanker was unable to transit the Bay of Biscay, being damaged by an air attack and forced back to Bordeaux on two occasions. It was then planned that another tanker, the *U-487*, would refuel the group south of the Azores but she could not be found by the deploying submarines. It later transpired that she had been sunk by aircraft from the US carrier *Core*. In the end the outgoing *Monsun* boats were refuelled in a complicated set of manoeuvres by other U-boats diverted from their patrols, but by then three of the boats had also been sunk by air attack while a fourth – the *U-516* – returned to Bordeaux having given over most of her fuel to two others.

One of the boats that had been sunk was the new Type IXD$_2$ *U-200* which had been ordered to carry out a special operation before entering the Indian Ocean. A small contingent of commandos of the *Brandenburg* Division were embarked and they were to be landed on the South African coast with the aim of inciting the Boers to revolt against the British. Thirteen days out of Kiel the submarine was caught on the surface by an Australian Liberator aircraft operating from a base in Iceland; the submarine was sunk with all hands.

The remaining five boats of the group proceeded south, rounded the Cape and, when south of Mauritius, met with the tanker *Brake* which had been sent from Penang. The boats then separated and went on to their individual operating areas. The *U-168* (*Kapitänleutnant* Helmuth Pich) went first to a position off Bombay, where she torpedoed and sank the British steamer *Haiching* on 2 October and also sank six sailing vessels by gunfire. Pich then took his boat to the Gulf of Oman but had no further success before heading for Penang, which he reached on 11 November.

The *U-183* (*Kapitänleutnant* Heinrich Schafer) had been given an area between the Seychelles and the African coast but had no success there and reached Penang at the end of October. On arrival Schafer, who was sick, was relieved by Fritz Schneewind who had earlier delivered the *U-511* to the Japanese. Sadly, Schafer never recovered and died in Singapore three months later.

The *U-188* (*Kapitänleutnant* Siegfried Ludden) was off the Horn of Africa at the end of September when the American ship *Cornelia P Spencer* was torpedoed and sunk. A few days later Ludden made an unsuccessful attack on a convoy leaving the Gulf of Oman, a failure which was attributed to the deterioration – due to the heat in the tropics – of the batteries in the electric torpedoes, causing them to run too slow. Ludden then cruised down the west coast of India before reaching Penang on 30 October.

The *U-532* (*Fregattenkapitän* Otto-Heinrich Junker) was the most successful of the *Monsun* boats at this stage. After leaving the refuelling area south of Mauritius Junker headed towards the west coast of India and, between the 19 September and 20 October, torpedoed and sank three ships, sank another with torpedo and gunfire, and damaged another in a torpedo attack on a convoy. The *U-532* also reached Penang on 30 October.

Fate was not kind to the remaining boat of the group, the *U-533* (*Kapitänleutnant* Helmut Hennig). After refuelling Hennig went north to the Gulf of Oman, where the submarine was sighted by a Bisley aircraft of the RAF[13] which dropped four depth charges as the submarine was submerging. There was just one survivor who was picked up after twenty-eight hours in the water.

The four boats newly arrived in Malaya joined the *U-178*, which had reached Penang from an earlier patrol in the Indian Ocean. Her commander, *Korvettenkapitän* Wilhelm Dommes, who was in ill health, was appointed to run the new base and command of the *U-178* was given to *Kapitänleutnant* Wilhelm Spahr.

Earlier the *U-511* (*Kapitänleutnant* Fritz Schneewind) had arrived in Penang on 7 August and had been transferred to the Japanese Navy. Sailing with the submarine from Germany had been Vice-Admiral Naokuni Nomura, who had represented Japan on the tripartite military commission in Berlin. This Type IXC U-boat became the *RO-500* and sailed for Kure. The second U-boat to be handed over, the Type IXC_{40} U-1224, was manned by a Japanese crew which had been brought to Europe onboard the Japanese *I-8*. She became the *RO-501* on 15 February 1944 and sailed for the Far East in early March. On 13 May she was sunk in mid-Atlantic by an American destroyer. Vainly waiting for her at a pre-ordered fuelling position in the Indian Ocean was the *I-8*!

The results of this Eastern deployment of the *Monsun* Group were disappointing. Nine submarines and a U-tanker had set out. Four U-boats had been sunk, while a fifth had returned after giving its fuel to colleagues. The U-tanker had been damaged and forced to return; its replacement had been sunk. Only four boats had reached Penang after four months at sea, and between them they had sunk only eight ships and six small sailing vessels. It was not an auspicious beginning. The Germans were left with the need to maintain and resupply the submarines at Penang and also to reinforce their new flotilla.

Notes:

1 *Fuehrer Conferences on Naval Affairs*, Greenhill Books, 1990.

2 *The U-Boat* by Eberhard Rossler, Arms & Armour Press 1981.

3 The Americans are often criticised for this attack carried out by a B-25 Mitchell bomber. In 1963, Brigadier General Robert C. Richardson USAF stated in an interview in NATO HQ: 'I gave the order to bomb the *Laconia* survivors. We did not know there were British among them. But, even if we had, it would have made no difference, I would have given the order anyway.'

4 *War in the Southern Oceans* by L. Turner and others.

5 *Wings of the Dawning* by Arthur Banks.

6 HMS *Statesman*, for example, fired nearly 500 rounds of 3 inch ammunition during the course of one patrol. See Chapter Nine.

7 Details from the *U-181*'s log supplied to the author by Mr Bob Coppock of the Naval Historical Branch.

8 Type XIV: length 22½ feet; 1,688/1,932 tons displacement; range 9,300 miles at 12 knots; no torpedo armament but carried four spare torpedoes for replenishment in pressurised containers aft of the conning tower. 432 tons extra fuel carried for refuelling. Ten boats of this type were completed; all were sunk.

9 *Leonardo da Vinci*: 251 feet in length; 1,195/1,490 tons displacement; range 2,900 miles at 17 knots or 10,500 miles at 8 knots surfaced; armament eight 533mm (21 inch) torpedo tubes – four forward, four aft – sixteen torpedoes and one 100mm gun. Five of the six boats of this class were lost in operations in the Atlantic, the *da Vinci* being the most successful Italian submarine.

10 *The Japanese Submarine Force in World War II* by Carl Boyd and Akihiko Yoshida.

11 *Wings of the Dawning* by Arthur Banks.

12 'Problems of Leadership' – originally delivered as a lecture to many senior officers of the *Wehrmacht* and the Nazi Party elite in 1943.

13 The Bristol Bisley was a modified version of the Blenheim Mk 5.

Nine
The British – Final Patrols

Until early 1944 targets for the British and Dutch submarines patrolling off the Malay coast were almost exclusively coasters and small merchant ships; major Japanese warships were not seen after the successes of HMS *Templar* and *Tally Ho* in January and February. Between January 1944 and the end of the war German or Japanese U-boats were sighted on twenty-one different occasions, but except in three cases the Allied submariners were either unable to reach a firing position or their torpedoes had missed. One of these boats was HMS *Thule* (Lieutenant Alastair Mars), which attacked an 'RO' class submarine on 28 December 1944 with a stern salvo of three torpedoes when on patrol off Penang. On hearing an explosion Mars raised the periscope and was rewarded with the sight of a large column of water in line with the target and could see the stern of the Japanese submarine rising steeply. He was convinced that his target had been sunk. Later, it was learned that the magnetic firing pistol had activated prematurely and in fact what Mars had seen was the Japanese boat carrying out one of the fastest 'crash dives' ever.

One of the successes occurred in July 1944 when the *Telemachus* (Commander Bill King) was patrolling off the One Fathom Bank. After a night on the surface recharging her batteries the *Telemachus* dived just before dawn on the 17th. Later that morning a large Japanese submarine was sighted steering southwards, the steady course being predictable because of the narrowness of the channel at that point. King fired a spread of six torpedoes at 2,000 yards range. The enemy submarine blew up and there were no survivors. Later, intelligence showed that this was the *I-166*[1] (Lieutenant Commander Suwa) en route to Singapore for repairs. Earlier that morning the same submarine had been sighted by the *Tantulus* but an attack had to be broken off when the Japanese boat altered course. As a result of the sinking both British boats were hunted by the Japanese in the subsequent anti-submarine activity.

In September the *Trenchant* (Lieutenant Commander Arthur Hezlet) also made a successful attack, this time on a U-boat entering Penang.[2] Just one hit from a three torpedo stern salvo was sufficient to send *Kapitänleutnant* Johann Jebsen's *U-859* to the bottom. Some twenty survivors were left swimming on the surface; the *Trenchant* picked up eleven of these and took them back to Ceylon, leaving the remainder to be picked up by a Japanese destroyer which was sighted approaching the area.

Hezlet was faced with a serious problem. The *Trenchant* was already crowded with her full crew and some Special Forces personnel; now there were an additional eleven German prisoners to be accommodated – and guarded. The Germans were distributed among the various messes and, although the prisoners proved to be no trouble, Hezlet issued pistols to some of the crew, retaining one for himself. As experienced submariners the Germans had the potential to cause damage to the submarine and they had to be accompanied at all times.

To keep the Germans occupied they were given cleaning duties, one of which was to assist with dumping rubbish overboard at night. Commander Hezlet remembers one occasion:

> *... a Petty Officer of the Watch who used to wear his pistol on his waist, like a cowboy. On one refuse dump he was casually sauntering along, with two of the POWs directly behind him carrying buckets of refuse. They could so easily have disarmed him.*[3]

A more useful service was carried out by another of the Germans. The *Trenchant*'s water distiller was a machine of German origin, and had produced minimal amounts of fresh water for the expenditure of a great deal of electricity. The German, who had operated a similar machine onboard the *U-859*, was able to coax better results from the equipment.

On return to Trincomalee the Germans were disembarked to the *Adamant* before being handed over to the Army. The only officer, *Oberleutnant* Horst Klatt, was sent to a POW camp in Egypt and did not return to Germany until 1948.

As more British submarines became available for operations it was possible to send them to patrol off the west coast of Sumatra to attack Japanese shipping using those waters. One such patrol was made in September 1944 by HMS *Tradewind* (Lieutenant Commander Lynch Maydon). First the submarine landed two agents on the coast of Sumatra and then went further south to contact an agent in the vicinity of the southern entrance to the Sunda Strait. Contact could not be made and Maydon left the area fearful that the agent had fallen into the hands of the

The gun crew of a 'T' class submarine in action. The submarine is trimmed down ready to dive and the fore planes are turned out.

Japanese. Almost the entire patrol was carried out with the handicap of the main search periscope being flooded. Despite this an escorted enemy merchant ship, later found to be the *Junyo Maru*, was sighted on 18 September and after a brief attack was sunk with two torpedo hits. Later two barges carrying cement were intercepted, boarded and then sunk with demolition charges. The *Tradewind* returned to Trincolmalee on 4 October. It was not until later that it was found that the *Junyo Maru* was carrying nearly 6,000 American, British and Dutch POWs; few survived the sinking.

By May 1944 it had become evident that the Japanese were using junks of varying sizes, in addition to the limited number of coastal vessels, to carry essential supplies from Malaya to their armies in Burma. As a consequence submarines were given permission for these craft to be attacked. Many of the junks were too small to merit the expenditure of even a single torpedo and had to be attacked using either the 3 inch or 4 inch gun with which the submarine was fitted.

One gun action by the *Taurus* could have ended disastrously. The submarine was patrolling off Port Blair in the Andaman Islands. It was a dreary business. The Rising Sun flag could be seen flying from the flagstaff of what had been Government House; aircraft took off and landed from the airfield to the south, but proved to be no threat to the submarine. Occasionally smoke was seen rising from the harbour, but no ships were visible to the eye of the periscope watchkeeper. The area might have been deserted. There was, however, one recurring incident that provided some interest. Every other day a small steam ferry arrived at about mid-day and left again in the evening. With no other targets to be found the Commanding Officer, Lieutenant Commander Mervyn Wingfield, decided to stop this ship and find out where it came from, where it went, and what it was carrying.

One of the submarine's officers, Lieutenant John Gibson, describes the scene in great detail.[4]

We worked out a plan of campaign. When the ship arrived we would cut him off and surface across his bow, threatening him with instant destruction should he not stop. Two of our men with line grapnels would make the ferry fast to our hull, putting it between us and any watchers on the shore. Then we would steam out to sea and examine the prize in our own time. The boarding party would be armed with revolvers, tommy guns, grenades and explosive charges. We had with us on this patrol a Captain in the 'Cloak and Dagger' Brigade, who had come along in case we had to go in and search for the Major and his party [landed during an earlier patrol]. *He was mad keen to get a little action, so we made him Boarding Officer. That job was always reserved for passengers.*

Punctually the next day the ferry arrived on the scene and we sped along under water to put ourselves in the right position. It was found that the enemy was doing a fair turn of speed, and in the end we had to surface and chase her, trying to stop her with a few rounds from the gun. The first round knocked away a little privy from the stern. After a few near misses the ferry stopped and we dashed up, our party of desperadoes standing by on deck. As we swung alongside her the enemy was secured by grapnels in age-old fashion, but before our men could get aboard a party of eighteen Indians had turned the tables and boarded us. They were quite friendly and pointed at the ferry, drawing their fingers across their throats. There were clearly some Japs in the ship.

Then everything happened fast. The forward grapnel came adrift, and as our men began to get aboard the ancient steamer she swung round and lay across our stern. A small boat, not previously seen, approached from the port side, and in it we could see a bland Chinaman rowing steadily towards us. In the bows of the dinghy sat a sleek-looking Japanese officer. We held our breath, and in a second that man was covered by every available weapon. Here was our chance for a prisoner.

The Jap suddenly crouched low over the gunwale, his bared teeth shone in the sunlight. He was holding something to his stomach; perhaps he was going to slice it open. There was a gold watch on his wrist; his hair was neatly brushed, very black against the skin of his flat forehead. Only a few feet separated him from the green of our hull. One of our men went down to get hold of the little boat. Suddenly the

Japanese officer leapt at the Chinaman, slashed madly, and dived into the clear water. Without order, without being led, all our gunners opened fire on that black head in the water. The line of bullets cut along the calm surface until there was a pool of blood where the head had been. We had lost our prisoner.

In those few minutes the situation changed all round. Our boarding party was aboard the ferry, but someone put her engines to full ahead and the last grapnel parted with a 'ping'. The ferry headed off towards Port Blair with smoke billowing from her funnel. On her decks we could see our men wrestling with the steering, trying to get her back alongside. The Indians were clambering over the submarine; one of them could speak just enough English to say: 'Jap, no good. No good.' He would then draw his finger over his throat for the hundredth time. There was no time to listen. The submarine was only two miles off the harbour entrance and at any moment aircraft or chasers could arrive. In the meantime our boarding party in the ferry were chasing round the water, having a great time.

If we had not known that there was a battery of 6-inch naval guns about six thousand yards to the south west we might have been amused by the situation. In actual fact it was pretty scary, but there was enough ballyhoo going on to make us shrug our shoulders and smile. For five minutes the picture remained the same. There on the sun-baked surface lay the submarine, her decks crowded with a mass of grinning and chattering Indians. Away over the water the ferry with our men aboard was still going round in circles, while beyond them we could see the Japanese flag blowing out in the light breeze. The buildings ashore shimmered in the haze. It appeared the enemy were having an afternoon sleep.

At the end of a tense five minutes the ferry straightened up and headed towards us. At the same time we sighted an aircraft coming out from the airfield. It was a race against time. As the ferry hit us with a bang and our men leapt aboard, the Captain pressed the diving klaxon. The boarding party broke all speed records as they raced for the bridge, the last man jumping down the hatch just as the water swished aboard. The poor Indians were left up there, but they had the little dinghy near them, and the ferry was still churning around in the vicinity. The bombs arrived while we were still at thirty feet, going down fast. It was a pretty near thing.

The general shortage of targets in their patrol areas resulted in the submarine crews having to work very hard for comparatively little reward. Targets were usually small and sailed close inshore in waters that were barely deep enough for the submarine to dive, and which were far too shallow for comfort should the submarine be attacked. The Japanese became masters of camouflage, their junks being covered with a veritable array of foliage and palms, often only betraying their presence to a waiting submarine by unnatural movement and change of bearing. Often the junks would be found to be carrying nothing more than a mere 20 tons of rice, coal or foodstuffs, a lighter would be loaded with 1,000 or more

Lt Cmdr M.R.G. Wingfield, DSO, DSC, RN and Lt J.F. Gibson, RNVR. (RN Submarine Museum)

gallons of petrol, while sighting a coaster of 500 tons was a real event, but even these small amounts in each vessel were vital to the Japanese troops in Burma who were desperately short of supplies.

The Malay or Chinese crews of these vessels were found to be remarkably sanguine about the fate of their craft. Co-operation was frequent as they abandoned their junk before clambering into a small boat and heading for the shore. Occasionally it was possible to gather the crews of several junks together and place them in one large craft in which they could be sent shorewards. Seldom were any Japanese guards found to be onboard these small craft.

The wooden construction of the junks made them difficult to sink by gunfire; the shells would go straight through without exploding, so that it required a large number of hits to have the desired effect. It was found easier to board the junk and place demolition charges. Ironically, it was reported that this practice was less popular with the Chinese crews, who liked to gamble on the number of rounds required to sink their craft!

A gun action could go seriously wrong, as happened to the *Shakespeare* (Lieutenant David Swanston) in early January 1945 during her first patrol off Port

Blair. Swanston had already attacked and sunk the 2,500 ton *Unryu Maru* with a salvo of torpedoes. A second ship of the same convoy escaped, while the escorting destroyer's counter-attack was too far away to be of any discomfort to the submariners. On 3 January Swanston attacked and missed another small steamer with a second salvo. As there was no air cover or escorting destroyer in sight the *Shakespeare* surfaced and immediately attacked with the gun. It was shortly before eight o'clock in the morning. The 3-inch gun quickly scored one or two hits on the enemy's waterline but the Oerlikon jammed. At that moment a Japanese escort was seen approaching about $4\frac{1}{2}$ miles away and Swanston decided to dive, but before he could do so the enemy merchant ship scored a hit on the submarine, penetrating the pressure hull on the starboard side. Water poured into the control room and engine room and flooded the wireless office.

The *Shakespeare* was unable to dive and could only fight it out on the surface. The gun was manned again and fire was reopened on the enemy, who continued to fire at the submarine. The submarine was hit four more times before the enemy gun was silenced. Two of the submarine's gunners were wounded during the action, and two more members of the crew were wounded while they were attempting to plug the holes in the pressure hull with blankets. By this time the

The hole in the superstructure of HMS Shakespeare *caused by a Japanese shell. The Commanding Officer, Lieutenant David Swanson, is standing to the left. (RN Submarine Museum)*

second Japanese vessel was within range and it opened fire briefly on the submarine, but then inexplicably broke off the action and escorted the merchant ship into Port Blair.

With the wireless unusable it was impossible to call for help and, though the enemy appeared to have left the area, Swanston realised it was only a matter of time before the *Shakespeare* was attacked again. There was a hole some nine inches by four in the pressure hull and, in addition to the wireless being out of action, the gyro compass was also useless and the main ballast pump – the only effective way of getting water out of the submarine – was flooded and could not be used. A bucket chain had to organized. Then one engine seized and speed was reduced to seven knots.

At 9.30 the Japanese returned. A seaplane made a low level run from astern over the submarine and dropped a bomb about 20 yards away. The aircraft was given a good burst from one of the machine guns and caught fire, crashing into the sea about half a mile from the submarine. Thirty minutes later two more Japanese aircraft appeared, dropped two small bombs each, strafed the submarine and left. There were five more similar attacks during the morning and early afternoon.

When another enemy escort vessel was sighted the crew of the *Shakespeare* thought that this must surely be the end; confidential books were bagged and made ready to be thrown overboard, while patrol orders, signals and charts were burned. Strangely, however, the enemy ship made no attempt to engage or close the submarine; its actions have never been explained.

By sunset the submarine had survived twenty-five air attacks; fifty bombs, varying in size up to 1,000 lbs, had all missed. The men on the bridge had repeatedly been drenched by the splash of near misses; seventeen of them had been wounded by splinters or by machine gun or cannon fire, two of them fatally. Overnight the guns were stripped and cleaned, while down below work continued to reduce the level of water and to make good some of the many defects.

At dawn the following day the expected air attacks by the Japanese did not materialise. Knowing that HMS *Stygian* was due soon in that area, Swanston set a course which he hoped would intercept the other submarine. He hoped to make contact at about midnight on the 5th. The submarine was heeled to increase the height of the hole above water, though speed had to be reduced by another two knots. Incredibly, the engineers managed to weld a patch over the hole using the steel bridge chart table and various other items from around the submarine. Though it did not enable them to dive, it did stop any more water entering the boat. Best of all, while they made their way ever further towards safety, the sky remained clear of the enemy.

Eventually a rendezvous was effected early on the 6th with the *Stygian*, whose

As targets became smaller and fewer there was less demand to carry torpedoes and a need for increased stowage of gun ammunition. Here storage for 4 inch shells has been constructed in the torpedo stowage space of a 'T' class submarine. (RN Submarine Museum)

Commanding Officer, Lieutenant Guy Clarabut, was a personal friend of Swanston. Clarabut was cautious about this unheralded meeting and confirmation that all was well was only made when the two commanding officers exchanged the Christian names of their wives. Clarabut sent across some fresh food and some men to help with the repairs, then escorted his friend towards Trincomalee. *Stygian* also transmitted details of the action and the names of the casualties to the depot ship, HMS *Wolfe*. Later the destroyer HMS *Raider* appeared and took over the task of escorting the damaged submarine so that the *Stygian* was able to resume her patrol. The *Shakespeare* finally secured alongside the *Wolfe* on the 8th, five days after the action which so nearly destroyed her had started. She was considered unfit for further service.

The submarine is a weapon of stealth, preferring to make a silent unobserved approach and then deal a mortal blow to its prey with a salvo of torpedoes. The gun was intended only as a secondary form of attack. The peculiarities of submarine warfare off the Malayan coast in 1944 and 1945 changed these preconceptions. The shortage of torpedo targets and the increased number of gun actions highlighted two unforeseen design faults in the British submarines. When the 'T' class boats were first designed there was a requirement to keep topweight to a minimum in order to increase stability. As a consequence the gun platform was constructed with only waist high protection. The early submarines of this class arriving in the Far East had this inadequate arrangement and shipwrights onboard the depot ships had to manufacture their own rather crude half shields to provide the gun crews with some shelter from enemy fire. Many of the 'S' class – like the American, German and Japanese submarines – had no protection from return fire whatsoever, the guns being mounted in the open on the submarine's casing. Mention has already been made of the high ammunition expenditure by some boats. When originally designed the magazine of a 'T' class submarine was expected to carry a maximum of fifty 4 inch shells, an 'S' class somewhat less. As the war progressed boats were going to sea without their full outfit of reload torpedoes, carrying instead additional ammunition in locally made racks in the fore ends.

The experience of the *Statesman* (Lieutenant R.G.P. Bulkeley) in April 1945 clearly illustrates the way submarine warfare off the Malay coast had become very different from the accepted view of stealthy torpedo attack. She sank an entire convoy of seven landing craft, six by gunfire and the last by demolition charge after the Japanese crew had abandoned their vessel. Later in the patrol she sank a schooner, eight junks and three more landing craft. This was achieved by the expenditure of 493 rounds of 3-inch ammunition and countless rounds from the Oerlikon and the Vickers machine guns. No torpedoes were fired.

In February 1945 the submarines *Trenchant* (Commander A.R. Hezlet – newly promoted to that rank) and *Terrapin* (Lieutenant R.H. Brunner) operated in adjacent areas in the Malacca Straits and between them sank several targets, all with the gun. Then on 4 March they combined to attack and sink a submarine chaser in an action which completely exhausted the *Terrapin*'s ammunition. That night rubber boats took across sixty rounds from the *Trenchant* to her sister submarine. In return the *Terrapin* was able to send across 1,200 fresh duck eggs, which had been aboard one of the sunken junks, destined for Japanese Army. These became a welcome addition to the submariners' diet.

With the increase in gun actions by the submarines there was one other added imposition – the demand by Headquarters, back in the safety of Ceylon or India, for Japanese prisoners to be brought back. The code under which a Japanese serviceman fought was such that he would rather die for the Emperor than be taken prisoner, the latter bringing disgrace not only on the man himself but also upon his entire family. The land war in Burma led to very few enemy soldiers being brought in for interrogation; consequently submarine patrol orders included the instruction that, if possible, prisoners should be brought back from vessels which were sunk.

A submarine is not the best place to keep prisoners. There is no compartment

Gun crew of HMS Statesman *in action. (RN Submarine Museum)*

where they can be locked up, and it means that a member of the submarine's crew has to be taken from his normal duties to act as a guard. For the prisoner the opportunity to cause damage is there for the taking. As described earlier, Lieutenant Commander Arthur Hezlet in the *Trenchant* had enough trouble managing the eleven German prisoners that he had picked up; Japanese prisoners constituted a much greater potential for danger because of their fanaticism.

The *Taurus*, after sinking one ship by gunfire, found a number of survivors in the water, six of them Japanese. Some were wounded. The submarine approached the group but they made no attempt to swim towards it. They took no notice when lines were thrown to them to help them aboard and, raising their hands in the air, simply sunk from sight. Two of them deliberately swam into the propellers. When the British sailors turned their attention to the Malay survivors, the remaining Japanese tried to kill them also. The exception was one small Japanese sailor, who called out and began swimming towards the submarine, closely followed by one of his shipmates intent on preventing the Emperor's honour being defiled. Although wounded, the small sailor won by a short head and was hauled aboard the submarine, leaving his pursuer screaming in the water.

On the way back to Trincomalee the wounded Japanese sailor began to weaken, despite the best efforts of the *Taurus*'s Coxswain to look after him and dress his wounds. The authorities in Ceylon were so keen to have a prisoner that two Motor Torpedo Boats carrying a doctor and an interpreter were sent to rendezvous with the submarine to give the rescued sailor professional care.

The *Storm* (Lieutenant Commander E. Young RNVR) was another submarine which was able to bring back a prisoner. This one was uninjured and lived under armed guard in the fore ends with the sailors. It was found that he was a soldier rather than a sailor and his home town was Kobe, but otherwise the language barrier prevented any attempt to obtain information. He was made to scrub the decks throughout the boat every morning and did the job without complaining – and more thoroughly than was usual when the submarine was at sea! Another prisoner, nicknamed 'Tojo' by the crew of the submarine which had rescued him, spent his time polishing a multitude of valve handles, which had been made by the shipbuilders of a dull metal rather than the usual brass. He seemed reluctant to leave when the submarine reached harbour and found the army guards much less sympathetic than the sailors with whom he had lived as he was hustled away to an uncertain captivity.

Except for some special operations British submarines did not carry a doctor, unlike the German boats operating in the Indian Ocean far from their bases. For the British the font of medical knowledge in a submarine was invariably the Coxswain, who was aided by a slim red-covered handbook. The book described the simplest illnesses with step by step instructions for dealing with them and had an easy diagnostic aide-mémoire for more complicated problems. The submarine carried a small supply of antibiotics, pills and potions, including morphia for serious emergencies. In general the vast majority of cases requiring the Coxswain's expertise were heat rash, boils and minor cuts or wounds. More serious cases involved keeping the patient's condition stable until the submarine's return to harbour, or breaking radio silence to seek outside help.

While on patrol the Engineer Officer of the *Telemachus* was badly hurt while working to repair a defective bearing on one engine. The Commanding Officer, Commander King, had to break radio silence and a rendezvous was arranged with a Catalina amphibian aircraft. The officer was safely evacuated but had to have his hand amputated. Had he remained onboard the submarine his eventual recovery would have been more doubtful.

For some strange reason it was decided in early 1944 that the little red book should be withdrawn, leaving submarines on patrol dependent on the past experience of their Coxswains or on increasing use of the radio for advice. This lack of the handbook had interesting consequences during the first patrol of HMS *Thule* (Lieutenant Alastair Mars) in November 1944. A number of the crew all went down with similar symptons: high temperature, shaking limbs, acute diarrhoea and stomach cramps. One rating died. With no practical advice at hand, Mars, his Coxswain and the Engineer Officer pooled their limited medical knowledge and came to the same conclusion – cholera. After a signal to

The wounded Engineer Officer of HMS Telemachus *is evacuated by a Catalina flying boat. (RN Submarine Museum)*

Trincomalee the *Thule* was ordered to leave patrol and rendezvous with the destroyer *Terpsichore*, which would bring out a doctor and a complete Spare Crew for the submarine. Fortunately, the doctor found no trace of cholera, only severe heat exhaustion.

The crews of the large American submarines were luckier that their British counterparts as each boat carried a 'Pharmacist's Mate'. With some medical training these crewmen were able to deal with most emergencies until the submarine returned to harbour – indeed, on more than one occasion they had to operate (successfully too) for appendicitis.

In August 1944 there was a change to the flotillas at Trincomalee. By then it was thought that there were too many submarines for the limited number of targets off the Malay and Sumatran coasts and northwards towards Burma. HMS *Maidstone* and the 8th Flotilla – three 'T' class, six 'S' class and the Dutch O 19 – were transferred to Fremantle in Western Australia under the operational command of the American Commander Submarines, South West Pacific. Their area of operations was the South China Sea, to the north of the archipelago of the Dutch East Indies, and so they form no further part of this story.

However, the submarines carried out a patrol of short duration en route to

Australia so that they could make the long passage to Fremantle without having to refuel. The *Maidstone* went direct, taking with her all the submarines' spare gear, reload torpedoes and the submariners' own kit. It was a complicated logistical problem to ensure that everything was in the right place at the right time.

A major worry for both the staff in Trincomalee and the patrolling submarines was to ensure that the boats could reach their billets without fear of attack from a friendly submarine, and could similarly leave in safety at the end of a patrol. Great care had to be taken by submarines in transit to keep to the correct navigational route and timings, the movements being made known to submarines already on patrol in adjacent areas.

It has already been recorded how this information had been used to advantage by Lieutenant Swanston in the *Shakespeare* to effect a rendezvous after his submarine had been badly damaged. On the other hand, the dilemma that this knowledge could cause is illustrated by an incident in the *Storm*. While proceeding dived to his patrol area Lieutenant Commander Young received a report from his asdic (sonar) operator that there were propeller noises, probably electric motors, passing down the port side. There was nothing in sight through the periscope. By using the asdic actively a 'ping range' of 4,500 yards was obtained. However, because Young knew that the *Tactician* was returning to Trincomalee at that time he took no action to initiate an attack. Later, he was able to confirm that it was the *Tactician*.

Before the year's end another submarine was lost. The *Stratagem* (Lieutenant C. Pelly) sailed for her fourth patrol and was given an area in the Malacca Strait by the One Fathom Bank. On 19 November a convoy of five merchant ships and three escorts was attacked, Pelly firing three torpedoes at a range of 2,500 yards at the second ship of the line. The *Stratagem* then went deep while the escorts conducted an ineffectual counter-attack, dropping about twenty depth charges. Returning to periscope depth, Pelly saw that his target was still afloat and fired his stern tube. The 2,000 ton Japanese cargo ship *Nichinan Maru* sank at once. The next day the *Stratagem* was sighted by an aircraft and then heavily attacked by a destroyer, leaving her severely damaged and beginning to flood. Lieutenant Douglas and seven other survivors escaped from the forward torpedo compartment of the submarine and were picked up by the destroyer and taken to Singapore. They were badly beaten and maltreated before being sent on to POW camps. Only Douglas and two others survived to be repatriated at the end of the war.[5]

From March 1944 the British submarines were also employed in an extensive minelaying campaign in the Malacca Straits and northward, off the west coasts of Thailand and southern Burma. The aim of these minefields was to force Japanese shipping away from the coast and into deeper water where it could be readily attacked by the submarines. By the end of the war 24 minefields had been laid in

HMS Stratagem. *(RN Submarine Museum)*

that area with an additional two fields laid in the approaches to Port Blair in the Andaman Islands. A total of 502 mines were laid,[6] mostly in groups of only 8 or 12, from the tubes of the 'S' and 'T' class submarines. The large minelayers *Porpoise* and *Rorqual* were able to lay up to 50 Mk XVI moored contact mines at a time from the special mining rails within the casing.

During the First World War six of the 'E' Class submarines had been built as minelayers capable of carrying twenty moored mines in vertical tubes in the midships saddle tanks. Later six of the 'L' Class were similarly built. In July 1920 the Naval Staff began an investigation into the need and requirement for submarine minelayers. The main controversy at that time was whether the mines should be carried internally or externally. At the time the Rear Admiral (S) – or Flag Officer Submarines as he later became known – was strongly against the idea of the 'internal minelayer' and as an experiment the obsolete monitor submarine, the *M3*, was converted to carry mines. Although not an operational success the *M3* proved the value of the minelayer carrying mines on a track inside the casing. This in turn led to the construction of the six submarines of the *Porpoise* class.[7]

Early in 1940 the submarine-laid magnetic ground mine was evolved, although it was 1942 before it came into service. These M Mark II mines were laid from the torpedo tubes of submarines and weighed 1,760 lbs, of which 1,000 lbs was the amatol charge.[8] Each mine was roughly half the length of a

A submarine of the Porpoise *class loading mines. Through the open stern door a mine can be seen on the rails which run the length of the submarine inside the casing. The offset periscopes are also clearly visible.*

torpedo enabling two to be carried in each reload position, though they could only be loaded and fired singly. The main drawback was that this left the submarine defenceless during the time the mines were being laid. The torpedoes had to be pulled back, the mines loaded and, after firing, a second salvo had to be loaded and fired before the torpedoes could be reloaded. The submarine had to be kept very carefully trimmed at periscope depth throughout all this activity as it was essential that the positions in which the mines were laid be accurately known. It was always a great relief when this part of the patrol had been successfully accomplished.

In terms of tonnage sent to the bottom it was not a spectacular campaign: only two small warships and five merchant ships were sunk. However, it undoubtedly caused the Japanese to divert scarce assets to the area to try and deal with the problem.

On 9 January 1945 the *Porpoise* (Lieutenant Commander H.B. Turner) confirmed that she had laid two minefields off Penang. On the 16th she was overdue at Trincomalee, having failed to answer any signals since the report of the minelay, and nothing more was ever heard from her. The cause of her loss

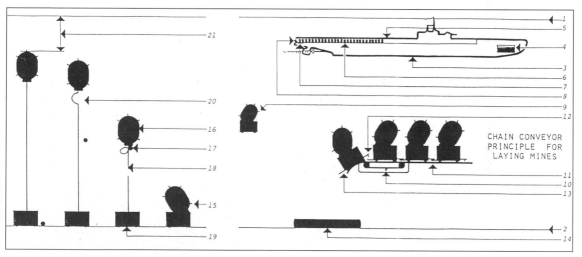

1 Surface of the sea. 2 Sea-bed. 3 Submarine laying mines. 4 Torpedo tubes loaded with ground mines. 5 Free-flooding casing holding mines. 6 Mines stored on rails. 7 Chain conveyor for shifting mines. 8 Mine released from submarine. 9 Mine descending to sea-bed. 10 Chain conveyor with hooks to haul mines. 11 Pin and bush coupling. 12 Coupling pin disengaged from bush. 13 Mine at after end of rails falling into the sea. 14 Ground influence mine resting on sea-bed. 15 Mine and sinker resting on sea-bed. 16 Mine ascending. 17 Hydrostat with 'loose bight'. 18 Mooring wire. 19 Sinker with mooring rope drum. 20 Hydrostat releases loose bight and falls clear; sudden break in tension causes mooring drum to lock mine at sea depth. 21 Set depth.

remains unknown; the Japanese made no claims for her sinking. She was the 75th and last British submarine to be lost during the war, the third in the Far East. Her sister ship, HMS *Rorqual* (Lieutenant J.P.H. Oakley), continued to be available to lay mines, and at the end of the war this veteran submarine was the sole survivor of a class of six which had been built before the war. During the war she laid a total of some 1,350 mines in 38 minelays.

By the end of 1944 the British and American Air Forces were able to launch long-range air raids on the Japanese in Thailand and even as far south as Singapore. From time to time the Fleet Air Arm operated against oil refineries in Sumatra. These raids inevitably resulted in aircraft losses and it was a great comfort to the airmen to know that at specific points on their route there would be a submarine waiting to pick them up should they be forced to ditch. As the war progressed and the threat from enemy aircraft diminished as the power of the Allied Air Forces grew, this 'plane-guard' duty, as it was known, was assigned to most Allied submarines at one time or another. In the Pacific the American submarines saved countless numbers of their airmen, while the British submarines from Ceylon performed an equally valuable task.

One such submarine was the *Seadog* (Lieutenant E. Hobson), on her first patrol. At the end of February 1945 she was in position to pick up four American airmen. Within hours a Catalina aircraft had landed alongside and the Americans were once more on their way, back to their base in India.

On another occasion an American pilot was rescued while under fire from shore batteries by the *Tactician* (Lieutenant Commander A. Collett) off Sabang, the operation becoming more hazardous for the submarine when an enemy torpedo boat was sighted

Submarines were constantly being called upon for Special Operations as preparations were made for the invasion to recover the Malay peninsular. The operations involved the landing or recovery of personnel, the landing of supplies and even simple beach reconnaissance. In 1944 and 1945, Special Operations were concerned in 48 of the 182 patrols carried out by the British submarines, and in 15 of those cases the clandestine nature of the operation precluded the submarine being involved in any offensive actions. The way in which Special Operations were conducted has already been described in detail with the work of the Dutch submarines.[9]

In October 1944 the *Trenchant* (Lieutenant Commander A.R. Hezlett) carried two 'chariots' for an operation in the harbour at Phuket Island. Quite simply, a chariot consisted of a torpedo-like device, twenty-five feet long, constructed to take two men riding astride behind protective shields. They wore cumbersome diving suits and had special breathing equipment which left no bubbles in the water. There was an explosive charge of about 700 lbs which formed the bow

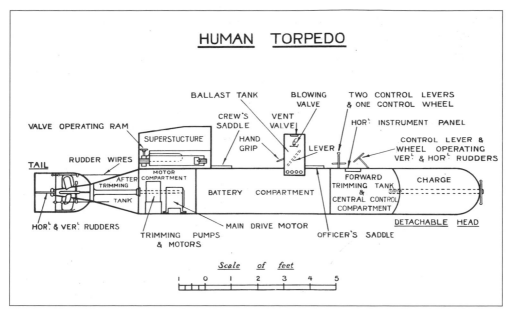

HUMAN TORPEDO

BALLAST TANK

BLOWING VALVE

TWO CONTROL LEVERS & ONE CONTROL WHEEL

CREW'S SADDLE

VENT VALVE

HOR⁼ INSTRUMENT PANEL

VALVE OPERATING RAM

SUPERSTUCTURE

HAND GRIP

LEVER

CONTROL LEVER & WHEEL OPERATING VER⁼ & HOR⁼ RUDDERS

TAIL

RUDDER WIRES

MOTOR COMPARTMENT

AFTER TRIMMING TANK

BATTERY COMPARTMENT

FORWARD TRIMMING TANK & CENTRAL CONTROL COMPARTMENT

CHARGE

HOR⁼ & VER⁼ RUDDERS

TRIMMING PUMPS & MOTORS

MAIN DRIVE MOTOR

OFFICER'S SADDLE

DETACHABLE HEAD

Scale of feet

1   0   1   2   3   4   5

Diagram showing the layout of an early Mark of British 'chariot'.

Chariots carried on the after casing of a 'T' class submarine before an operation in the Mediterranean. Two of the chariots have been retracted from their carrying position for maintenance. (RN Submarine Museum)

section of the chariot and could be detached and clamped magnetically to the target. The chariots had a range of about 20 miles and a top speed of a little over 4 knots.[10] They were taken near to their target by a conventional submarine, on which they were held in special mountings on the after casing. The moment of launch was the most dangerous time for the parent submarine as it had to surface to allow the crew of the chariot to embark and for the holding clamps to be released. The submarine then had to trim down by the stern for the chariot to be floated off. After launch each chariot and its crew made their own way for the final stage of the approach to the target. After an attack it was hoped that they would be able to return to the parent submarine where they could be picked up for the return journey. On arriving at their target one of the crew would 'dismount' and fix the explosive charge to the enemy ship while the second crewman kept the craft stable.

Chariots had been used to great effect on several occasions in the Mediterranean but many of the crews had been captured. The Italians had also achieved some spectacular successes against British targets. However, this was the first time that chariots had been used in the Far East – and it would also prove to be the last. One 5,000 ton merchant ship was sunk and a second badly damaged.[11] Following the attack both chariots successfully rendezvoused with the *Trenchant* and, after the crew had been taken aboard, the two small craft were scuttled. The operation had been a great success, but with the known brutality of the Japanese towards their prisoners it was considered that this method of attack presented a level of risk which was unacceptable and operations were suspended, reputedly on the direct intervention of Winston Churchill himself.

The 'S' and 'T' class submarines from Trincomalee continued to patrol off the Malay and Sumatran coasts until the end of the war. As the months went by targets became more and more scarce, the Japanese becoming increasingly reliant on small local craft to carry the limited supplies up the coast. The average length of a patrol was twenty-five days for a 'T' class and twenty days for an 'S' class. Even then it was a feat of endurance for the crews, who had to try to cope with the high temperatures and humidity. With the amount of fresh water severely restricted – about a gallon per man per day for all usage – it was only to be expected that they also had to accept the high incidence of prickly heat, boils and heat rash, yet overall the health and morale of the submariners remained good. The last submarine to return was the *Trident* (Lieutenant A.R. Profit), from what had been her 34th patrol. She had sailed for her first on 24 October 1939 and in between she had been on patrol in the Bay of Biscay and off the coast of Norway, had subsequently been based in Murmansk and had then seen service in the Mediterranean. The oldest submarine still in Royal Navy service at the end of the war was HMS *Clyde* (Lieutenant R.H. Bull), which had made a total of thirty-six patrols. She was completed in 1935 and returned from her last patrol, off the west coast of Siam, on 18 May 1945.

Notes:

1 The submarine *I-66* was completed in November 1932. The number was changed to *I-166* in May 1942.

2 For the third success in the period in which HMS *Tally Ho* sank the *UIT-23* in February 1944 see Chapter Seven.

3 Quoted from *Stalin's Silver* by John Beasant, Bloomsbury 1995.

4 Taken from *Dark Seas Above* by John Gibson, William Blackwood 1947.

5 Lieutenant Douglas' post-war report of the submarine's loss and his subsequent captivity is given in full as an Appendix to the Admiralty Staff *History of British Submarine Operations, Volume III*.

6 Details of the minefields laid by British submarines based on Trincomalee are listed in Appendix III.

7 *Porpoise* class: 289 feet overall; 1,768/2,053 tons displacement; speed $16/8\frac{1}{2}$ knots; range 11,500 miles at 8 knots surface, 66 miles at 4 knots dived; armament six 21 inch bow torpedo tubes, one 4 inch gun. Carried fifty moored mines.

8 *Naval Weapons of World War II* by John Campbell, Conways 1985.

9 See Chapter Four.

10 *Naval Weapons of World War II*.

11 The ex-Italian *Sumatra*, 4,859 tons, was sunk and the ex-Italian *Volpi*, 5,292 tons, was severely damaged.

Ten
Penang And After

In December 1941 the island of Penang was a quiet colonial centre for the British administration of the state of Penang, one of the Straits Settlements in what is now known as Malaysia. Its small port, Georgetown, was the second largest town in the colony, and was geared to cater for the ferry across to the mainland and for small vessels trading up and down the coast; it had no dockyard, no repair facilities and no berths for larger ships. Just ten days after the Japanese invasion of Malaya their troops were sweeping down the west coast and the island was abandoned by the British after only a few local demolitions. To add to the problems facing the British defenders, the entire fleet of local craft was controversially left undamaged, to be taken over – and used effectively – by the Japanese.

Even before the island and great naval base of Singapore had fallen to the advancing Japanese Army, the Japanese Navy had begun to prepare Penang's port for use as an advanced operational base. The 101st Detached Workshop of the Office of Naval Construction moved in to enable routine repairs and maintenance of small surface warships and submarines to be undertaken, although any major work would require a visit to the dockyard at Singapore – known to the Japanese as *Shonan*. In February 1942 the Workshop was expanded to become the base for a Japanese submarine flotilla. It has already been recounted how the Japanese submarines departed from Penang for their operational sorties into the Indian Ocean and for the long voyage to German occupied French ports.

By early 1943 Allied air and sea power was making it increasingly difficult for German blockade runners with their valuable cargoes to reach safety in French Atlantic ports. The Japanese submarine *I-30* had brought in some essential

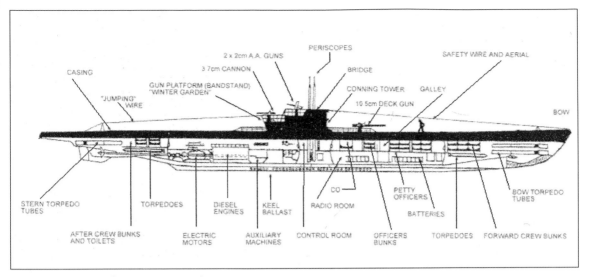

Diagram of Type IXD$_2$ U-boat.

material in its epic cruise of 1942, prompting consideration of the whole question of using U-boats as cargo carriers. The designed, but then unbuilt, Type XIX and Type XX U-boats were to be special cargo carrying submarines, the latter with a planned total capacity of 750 tons. Although building contracts for thirty Type XX boats were awarded, few were laid down and none were ever completed. Even the conversion of some Type VIIC boats, whereby 105 tons of cargo could be carried, was discussed, but the idea was not practicable as they had insufficient range to reach the Far East. In the short term the Type XB minelayers were available, since the special mines which they had been built to carry had proved unsatisfactory on trials.

As the rapid introduction of special transport U-boats was not feasible Admiral Dönitz proposed that the large Italian boats then operating in the Atlantic from Bordeaux should be converted to cargo carriers plying to and from the Far East. Another possibility that was considered involved the use of submarines which would proceed only through the Atlantic, where Allied airpower was predominant. The cargoes from several such boats could then be transferred to a single merchant ship off Madagascar to complete the voyage to Japan. Similarly a reverse procedure could be used for any cargoes from Japan. This was just one more desperate suggestion to resolve a difficult problem, the solution to which produced more questions than it answered.

After one or two difficulties the *Supermarina* (the Italian Admiralty) agreed in March 1943 that the ten Italian submarines then available at Bordeaux for operations in the Atlantic could be used as transports to the Far East, providing the Germans compensated the Italians by sending additional U-boats to the

Mediterranean. Two of the submarines concerned[1] were lost before they could be taken in hand for conversion, but the remainder were given the codename *Aquila* for this operation. Later, the Germans sought to include the two specially built transport submarines *Romolo* and *Remo*, as it was felt that there was by then no proper role for them in the Mediterranean following the Axis defeat in North Africa in June. The Italians refused, as they wished to keep these modern boats under their own command. By using the torpedo reload capacity it was hoped that the remaining eight Italian submarines would be able to carry up to 60 tons of cargo each to the Far East. In the event this was almost doubled. In addition, by converting every possible storage tank, provision was made for an extra 150 tons of fuel. At the same time that these alterations were being carried out in Bordeaux some of the bridge superstructure was removed to make the boats less conspicuous on the surface and to increase their stability. The attack periscope was also removed and a radar detection set installed.

After embarking their cargo the first two *Aquila* boats,[2] the *Barbarigo* and the *Enrico Tazzoli*, sailed for the Far East in May 1943 but were lost soon after departure. The next three submarines were more successful and by the end of August the *Reginaldo Giuliani*, the *Commandante Alfredo Cappellini* (*Tenente di Vascello* W. Auconi) and the *Luigi Torelli* had all reached Singapore. The first to arrive was the *Cappellini* after fifty-nine days at sea, low on supplies, her casing and superstructure damaged by atrocious weather south of the African coast and with many defects from the long voyage.

After effecting repairs the *Cappellini* was sent to Batavia to be loaded with 150 tons of rubber and 50 tons of tungsten, together with opium, quinine and spices. Auconi expected to be ready to sail for France in early September. The other two boats were also prepared with similar cargoes for the return passage. By then there was already doubt about Italy's ability to stay in the war and the Japanese authorities used every possible pretext to prolong the stay of the three Italian boats before they sailed for Europe. As soon as the news of the Italian capitulation was received the three Italian submarines were boarded by the Japanese and their crews taken away into captivity. The Japanese intended that the submarines should become part of the I.J.N., while the Germans expected to take the boats over themselves. After protracted negotiations between the two allies it was agreed that the boats should become German.

The Italian crew of the *Cappellini* were imprisoned in a camp in the jungle[3] in conditions similar to those endured by the many thousands of British and Australian POWs already held by the Japanese. The Italians were given the same pitiful rations and suffered the same brutal treatment as the soldiers of their erstwhile enemies. The other two crews were similarly incarcerated. As one-time allies of the Japanese the situation of the Italians was unusual, but their previous status did nothing to improve their living conditions. Whether it was as a result of representations by the German submariners in Penang or merely that the Japanese wished to be rid of these crews is not known, but *Tenente di Vascello* Auconi and his men boarded the 22,000 ton German blockade runner *Burgenland* in November 1943 just before the ship began its return to Europe. They were still prisoners, but their treatment was vastly improved. A few men from each crew preferred a sort of freedom and stayed to help man the Italian submarines for the Germans.

The *Burgenland* crossed the Indian Ocean safely but in January 1944, when midway between Ascension Island and the Brazilian coast, she was intercepted by the US cruiser *Omaha*. After the ship had been scuttled Auconi and his men found themselves sharing the same lifeboats as the German crew. Auconi himself took over command of one lifeboat from the German *Kapitän* Schmidt and successfully navigated it for nine days before reaching the Brazilian coast. The survivors remained as POWs in Pernambuco until the end of the war. Of the five fast merchant ships which left the Far East in the autumn of 1943, including the *Burgenland*, only one reached Bordeaux safely.

The submarines *Giuseppe Finzi* and the *Alpino Attilio Bagnolini* were held in Bordeaux until after the Italian capitulation in September, when they were taken over by the Germans. There was then further delay before they could sail as the German crews made themselves acquainted with the unfamiliar submarines, and it was January 1944 before the *Bagnolini*, by then known as the *UIT-22*, was ready to leave.

The *UIT-22* (*Oberleutnant* Karl Wunderlich) was bombed by aircraft in the South Atlantic, an attack which did not sink her but which caused her to lose so much fuel that she would have been unable to reach Penang. Arrangements were hurriedly made that she would meet the *U-178* (*Kapitänleutnant* Wilhelm Spahr), which was then returning to Europe from Penang, in order that she could receive more fuel. On arriving at the rendezvous 600 miles south of Capetown the *U-178* found only a large patch of oil and some wreckage. Only later did Spahr learn that the *UIT-22* had been bombed again the previous day and this time sunk, though not without causing damage to one of the Catalina aircraft involved. There were no survivors for the *U-178* to pick up.

The remaining submarine, the *UIT-21*, ex-*Giuseppe Finzi*, was found to have so many defects to her engines that it was necessary to pay her off and she was eventually scuttled in Bordeaux in August 1944, just before the port was captured by the Americans. It was not a propitious start for the programme of using submarines as cargo carriers for the Far East.

The Germans then had three submarines in the Far East for which they had virtually no crews. The problem was overcome by using some of the crew of the *U-511*, which had been handed over to the Japanese, some Italians who understandably preferred the idea of remaining loyal to Mussolini and working with the Germans to spending time as Japanese POWs, German civilians in the

Far East who were conscripted into the Navy, men from the crews of German ships in Japanese ports which were unable to sail for Europe, and even some soldiers. It was a far from perfect solution, but the only one possible. In any case the boats were not expected to have to carry out offensive operations and so could sail short-handed. However, before the boats could sail the new crews had to become acquainted with the submarines and trained to operate them safely.

The survivors of the first wave of *Monsun* boats reached Penang in the autumn of 1943. Before they arrived the base, which had been constructed by the Japanese for their own submarines, had to be substantially enlarged with additional workshops and maintenance facilities, accommodation for the crews and even a rest camp in the hills overlooking the town, where it was cooler. There was a shortage of skilled local labour, which meant that most of the maintenance work had to be undertaken by the German crews themselves at a time when they should have been resting after long patrols. Improvisation was often the order of the day. The task of setting up the base was at first overseen by *Fregattenkapitän* Wolfgang Ehrhardt, the former executive officer of the armed merchant cruiser *Michel*, then lying at Kobe in Japan. With the arrival of the *U-178 Korvettenkapitän* Wilhelm Dommes, who was in ill health, took over the administration of the base and the operation of the U-boats to be based there. Ehrhardt then became the senior German officer in the Malayan area, responsible not only for the German base in Penang but also detachments in Singapore, Batavia and Surabaya.

On the mainland the embryo British Imperial Airways base was taken over by the Germans for two Arado 196 single-engined seaplanes which had been removed from an armed raider in Japan. It was intended that these planes would fly anti-submarine patrols in the approaches to Penang whenever a U-boat was entering or leaving the port. Later, a Japanese Reichiki flying boat was added to the 'squadron'. The Japanese plane had been swapped for a *Bachstelze* taken from one of the Type IXD U-boats.

The British-built radio station in Penang enabled Dommes to keep in touch with Vice Admiral Wenneker in Tokyo, the U-boats in the Indian Ocean and, when conditions were right, with BdU in France or Germany. These radio signals were of course liable to interception and at certain stages of the war the messages could be decoded, giving the British vital information about the activities of the German submarines.

Reference has been made to the Japanese attitude to the Italian submariners once it was known that their Government had capitulated. Even as full allies the Germans found that their hosts were difficult to work with, though totally polite and correct in their responses. The problems of language were one reason for this; few Germans spoke any Japanese, while the reverse was hardly any better. One German officer records that at times the only common language was English! The Japanese officers made great efforts to entertain their German counterparts. Some 'international' sport was played but on the whole the German ratings looked after themselves and sport was restricted to that played between teams from individual submarines.

Of more interest to the Germans was the almost unnatural relationship between the Japanese Navy and the Army. On one occasion, with several German submarines in port, there was an enormous explosion in the harbour as a Japanese ammunition ship blew up. Instinctively the Germans rushed towards the scene of the accident and began dragging injured Japanese crewmen from the water. Others prepared their meagre medical supplies to give aid to the wounded. They were astonished at being ordered to leave the area by angry Japanese Naval Officers. Other Japanese officers and ratings were seen to be standing almost indifferently as they stared at the burning wreck. One officer became increasingly enraged as the German sailors ignored the orders to leave the area and continued to pluck badly burned men from the water. The senior German officer, *Korvettenkapitän* Dommes, was summoned to the office of the Japanese Island Commander, Admiral Uzuki, who explained that the accident had happened to an Army ship. It was therefore the duty of the Army to deal with the wounded and bury the dead; there was no reason for the Navy to become involved unless their Army colleagues specifically requested assistance.[4]

Another incident involved a U-boat arriving at the base. *Korvettenkapitän* Kentrat had already carried out one patrol in the Indian Ocean when he took the *U-196* out of Bordeaux on 16 March 1944 with orders to proceed to the Penang base after he had attacked any Allied shipping he could find in the Arabian Sea. He must have been very disappointed when he reached Penang some five months later having sunk just one ship, the *Shahzada*. Waiting to meet him was the Japanese Admiral and his staff, together with many of Kentrat's German comrades. It was pouring with rain as the submarine entered harbour and there was a strong off-shore wind which combined with the current to set the U-boat away from the jetty. Eventually Kentrat got the bow line across to one of the waiting German sailors, who put it around a nearby bollard. To everyone's surprise a Japanese Army private calmly walked up to the bollard and threw the line back into the sea. While the reception party waited in great discomfort the embarrassed Kentrat had to make another approach before berthing successfully. The Germans were surprised that the Admiral did not react. Subsequently they found that the part of the pier on which the bollard was situated belonged to the Japanese Army; as far as the private soldier was concerned no naval vessel – German or Japanese – had any right to use it.

For German U-boat commanders approaching Penang there was always the worry of an encounter with a British submarine and the temptation to relax their guard had to be resisted as they neared their destination. Both German and

Japanese authorities were also concerned about possible incidents should the U-boats be attacked by patrolling friendly aircraft, and the submarines were instructed to paint very clear identification marks on the casing and conning tower. On the front of the bridge a large vertical white stripe had to be painted; on each side a white roundel surrounding a black swastika. Across the forward casing another white stripe was to be displayed.

Dönitz ordered a second group of four submarines to leave for the Far East at the end of 1943. Of these, three were sunk in the Atlantic by Allied aircraft; only the *U-510* (*Kapitänleutnant* Alfred Eick) reached Penang, sinking five merchant ships during a short patrol in the Gulf of Aden and the Arabian Sea while on passage. Of the eleven ships claimed as sunk in this area during February and March 1944, eight were torpedoed by the *U-510*; of these, two were sunk and a third was damaged in an attack on a convoy approaching Aden escorted by only two minesweepers. As always with these deployments fuel was critical and Eick had to make two rendezvous during his five months at sea, the first with the Type XB *U-219*, which had been deployed as a tanker, west of the Cape Verde Islands, and then with the *Charlotte Schliemann* south of Mauritius.

The fuelling crisis was exacerbated in 1944 with the loss of the last two surface tankers in the Indian Ocean. The *Charlotte Schliemann* was sunk in February as a direct result of the decryption of intercepted German signal traffic ('Ultra'). The activities of the tanker had been known to the British for some time but it had not been possible to take any action on the information without risking a compromise of the fact that the German naval code had been broken. Finally, she was detected by the 'random' overflight of a Catalina aircraft which was able to call the destroyer HMS *Relentless* to the scene. The destroyer picked up the Captain and thirty-nine crewmen from the sinking ship before having to leave the area because she suspected that there were U-boats in the vicinity. Of the remaining crew, twelve men in one lifeboat reached Madagascar. After enduring twenty-seven days of privation, a second lifeboat was picked up by the *African Prince*. Two other boats were never found. The *U-532* (*Fregattenkapitän* Otto-Heinrich Junker) had been fuelling from the *Charlotte Schliemann* when the ship was first sighted by the aircraft but Junker escaped from the scene, managing to rescue a handful of the tanker's crew as he did so.

The tanker *Brake* was then ordered to the scene from Batavia. Once again the British were able to keep track of her movements through intercepted radio signals. On 12 March, as two U-boats were refuelling from her, the tanker was sighted by two Swordfish aircraft from the carrier HMS *Battler*. The destroyer HMS *Roebuck* was directed to the scene and sank the tanker with gunfire. In fact there were three U-boats present. The *U-188* and *U-532* had completed refuelling but the *U-168* had been forced to break off the operation as the four vessels sought calmer waters. All three boats dived as the aircraft approached, and remained so when the destroyer arrived to finish off the tanker. The log of the *U-188* (*Kapitänleutnant* Siegfried Lüdden) records the fact that the submarine had to remain dived and listen to the sounds of the bursting shells. The submarine had no torpedoes, having sunk six ships since leaving Penang, and so was unable to help as the battle went on for about an hour.

After the action the submarines surfaced and the survivors of the *Brake* were taken onboard the *U-168* (*Kapitänleutnant* Helmuth Pich) and back to Batavia. The conditions onboard the submarine in the tropical heat and with sixty-nine additional men onboard during the twelve days it took to reach port can only be imagined. The *U-188*, on the other hand, continued with her planned return to France. In late April she met with the southbound *U-181* and passed on all the latest information about conditions in the Indian Ocean and Penang. Lüdden successfully reached Bordeaux on 19 June, the first of the *Monsun* boats to return to France with a cargo of vital strategic materials.

Earlier one of the ex-Italian submarines, the *UIT-24* (*Oberleutnant* Heinrich Pahls), had left Penang with 180 tons of rubber, tin and other materials. She too had been due to refuel from the *Brake*. With the tanker sunk, she was forced to take sufficient fuel from the *U-532* to enable her to return to Penang. She had defects on her diesels and it would have been most unlikely that she could have reached France. In the enquiry held by BdU as to why the British had been able to intercept and sink two tankers in the remote ocean areas south of Mauritius, it was concluded that signals from the *UIT-24* had led the British to the area to sink the *Brake*, while the case of the *Charlotte Schliemann* could not be assessed. Nothing definite could be established and the secret of the decryption of the German naval codes by the British was narrowly kept.

The fate of Junker's *U-532* over the next few weeks clearly shows the complex organisation required to keep the U-boats at sea given that the only large surface tankers had been sunk. The submarine had left Penang to carry out a patrol in the Arabian Sea before setting sail for France. Besides her outfit of torpedoes she was carrying a cargo of tin, rubber, wolfram and molybdenum. After damaging one merchant ship and sinking another Junker effected a rendezvous with the *Charlotte Schliemann* to top up with fuel before setting off for Bordeaux, but was unable to complete this. After the tanker was sunk Junker remained in the area to fuel from the *Brake*, but again the replenishment was thwarted, leaving the submarine with insufficient fuel to reach France. She then gave fuel to the *UIT-24* to enable that boat to get back to Penang and later refuelled the *U-1062*, which was en route to Penang with a cargo of torpedoes. The *U-532* was then able to return to Penang herself.

The biggest worry for the boats in the Far East was the shortage of torpedoes. The Japanese torpedo was too long to fit in the torpedo tubes of the German submarines. In the Far East there were only a limited number of reloads, which had been taken from German armed raiders.[5] Dönitz's solution was to send two of the new Type VIIF U-boats to Penang. The design of this class of submarine, only four of which were ever built, was based on the Type VIIC but modified to carry additional torpedoes and extra fuel. In addition to the fourteen torpedoes carried for the boat's five tubes there was an additional compartment where a cargo of up to twenty-one torpedoes could be carried, with a further five in pressurised containers in the casing. To help these submarines when transiting the Atlantic, so heavily patrolled by Allied aircraft, a hinged *schnorkel* was fitted to the forward side of the conning tower, allowing the submarine to proceed submerged using its diesel engines. The *U-1062* (*Oberleutnant* Karl Albrecht) left Bergen for the Far East on 3 January 1944 and reached Penang on 19 April, having met the *U-532* to receive enough fuel to complete the passage. A sister ship, the *U-1059*, sailed in February for the Far East but was sunk by the Americans west of the Cape Verde Islands.

Dönitz continued to send boats to the Far East, a total of eleven setting out in early 1944. One of these was the veteran *U-181*, now under the command of *Kapitän zur Zee* Kurt Freiwald. The submarine arrived at Penang in August 1944 after carrying out a third patrol in the Indian Ocean during which she sank four merchant ships. In mid-July the submarine was caught on the surface by a Catalina aircraft and afterwards was hunted and depth charged for six hours by the sloop HMIS *Sutlej* and an aircraft, but Freiwald managed to slip away without suffering any significant damage. One night, as the submarine neared its destination, the lookouts sighted a dark shape off the port bow. For a few moments the conning tower of a British submarine remained in sight before it dived, and the *U-181* altered course away from the spot at full speed. The other submarine was HMS *Stratagem*, which tried to make a dived attack on the German boat but was unable to find its target through the periscope in the darkness.

Another submarine to set out at this time was the U-859 (*Kapitänleutnant* Johann Jebsen). This was a newly built boat and consequently she sailed from Kiel on 4 April, was routed north of Iceland and then southward into the Atlantic. Onboard, the submarine was crowded with supplies to last the crew over the long voyage to Penang; *Oberleutnant* Horst Klatt, the boat's Engineer Officer, remembered:

> *Even in their quarters the men could move about only on all fours, with food having to be eaten lying down. It was only towards the end of the long, difficult journey, when supplies for the crew stored in their quarters, which would usually have been kept elsewhere in the U-boat, were exhausted, that they were able to stand upright again.*[6]

In the early days of the voyage, while the submarine was in high Northern latitudes, the temperature in the boat rarely rose above 4°C and the only warm place to be found was in the engine room. When south west of Cape Farewell (southern tip of Greenland) Jebsen had his first success when he torpedoed and sank the Panamanian registered merchant ship *Colin*, a straggler from convoy SC157. As the submarine drove southward into the Atlantic the crew were constantly alerted to the fact that enemy air patrols were seeking German submarines, but Jebsen managed to avoid any contact. Further south the boat moved into tropical waters and the temperature onboard became unbearably hot, in stark contrast to those early days immediately after leaving their home port.

In late June the *U-859* moved into the Indian Ocean, but not without further discomfort. Off the Cape of Good Hope the submarine had met with a Force 11 gale which tossed the boat around like a toy, making life a nightmare for the bridge lookouts and terrifying for the remainder of the crew down below. The force of the storm damaged one of the guns mounted at the after end of the bridge and caused other damage to machinery. As the mountainous seas subsided the submarine surfaced south east of Durban to effect some repairs and to get rid of accumulated rubbish from below. At this time a Catalina aircraft dived on them from out of the early morning sun and dropped a total of five depth charges, one of which ruptured a fuel tank. In a second run the aircraft strafed the submarine, killing one rating and badly wounding an officer. The aircraft then left the area, having been hit by return fire.

The *U-859* crept away from the area where it had been attacked and then turned north to begin operations in the Arabian Sea. During this time Jebsen evaded the attentions of two frigates, HMS *Barth* and *Tay*, which added to his worries about the effect the length of this patrol was having on the health and fitness of his crew. The submarine was still in contact with home through a giant radio transmitter in Germany which broadcast news and other programmes designed to maintain the morale of crews long parted from the Fatherland. It was in this way that the crew heard the sensational news of the 20 July assassination attempt on the life of Adolf Hitler. Few of the crew were actual members of the Nazi Party but nevertheless the news had a profound effect on them.

On 27 August the *U-859* reported that it had sighted and torpedoed a British tanker, though post-war analysis fails to identify or confirm this claim. On the following night three torpedoes sent the *John Barry* to the bottom and on 1 September the *Troilus* was sunk, after which Jebsen decided to head for Penang. The *John Barry* was important because of its secret cargo of over a million and half silver coins, some of which were salvaged in a remarkable operation in 1992.[7] The voyage of the *U-859* ended off the port of Penang on 23 September, when a torpedo from HMS *Trenchant* sank the submarine almost instantaneously, leaving only eleven of the crew to be picked up by the British submarine and another eight to be rescued by the Japanese. The story of the voyage and the subsequent loss of the *U-859* so near to Penang after 175 days at sea has been told in some detail to illustrate some of the conditions which the German submariners had to endure on passage to and from the Far East.[8]

Of the U-boats that had reached the Far East only two were operational – the *U-861* and the *U-862* – in late 1944 and early 1945. Eight more lay in various ports, either undergoing maintenance and repair or being loaded for a return to Europe. The *U-862* (*Korvettenkapitän* Heinrich Timm) made the last successful patrol of these submarines. In a patrol that must rank as the most distant of all for a U-boat, she ranged as far as the northern tip of New Zealand and circumnavigated Australia, sinking one ship off Sydney on Christmas Eve 1944 and then another off Perth in February. In the Australian Bight, south of Adelaide, Timm attempted to sink the Greek merchant ship *Ilissos* by gunfire, but heavy seas and accurate return fire by the merchant ship's gunners forced the U-boat to dive and the Greek ship managed to escape into a heavy rain squall. The mystery is that so few ships were encountered by Timm.

The *U-183* (*Kapitänleutnant* Fritz Schneewind) left Batavia in April to operate off the Philippines, the Japanese having finally consented to German requests for their experienced submariners to attempt to disrupt the American build-up of resources as they advanced towards the Japanese mainland. The submarine was

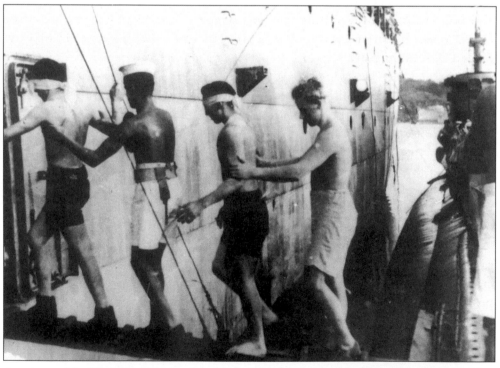

Survivors of the U-859 being transferred from HMS Trenchant *to the submarine depot ship in Trincomalee before being taken away to POW camps. (John Beasant)*

sighted in the Java Sea by the USS *Besugo* (SS-321), commanded by Lieutenant Commander Herman Miller, which was on patrol off Surabaya. At the time the *U-183* was flying a Japanese flag and it was not until Miller surfaced to pick up the lone survivor that the nationality of the other submarine was established.

The *U-861, U-510* and the *U-532* were all sailed for Europe as soon as they could be made ready. The *U-861* (*Korvettenkapitän* Jurgen Oesten) sailed from Surabaya in January 1945 with a cargo of strategic supplies which included 100 tons of zinc. Successfully evading all Allied air and sea patrols, Oesten put into Trondheim in Norway on 19 April, only to have to surrender to the British when they occupied the port in early May. The submarine then had to be taken to join many other surrendered U-boats at Lissahally in Northern Ireland, but the British did not have the expertise to undertake the passage and sought the help of Oesten and his crew. Eventually it was agreed that the Germans would sail for Ireland and would be repatriated on arrival. Sadly, higher authority decreed otherwise and as soon as Oesten and his crew reached Lissahally they were immediately made prisoners of war – or 'prisoners of peace', as Oesten prefers to call the experience.

The *U-510* (*Korvettenkapitän* Alfred Eick) had sailed for home at the end of November 1944 but had been forced to return to Batavia only a week later with engine trouble. The *U-510* left Batavia for a second time in mid-January 1945, also bound for Norway and then a German port. Eick torpedoed and sank the *Point Pleasant Park* near Capetown in February, crossed the equator in March and evaded all hunting patrols, but shortage of fuel forced Eick to put into St Nazaire on 24 April. There the boat was surrendered to the French when they reoccupied the port at the end of the war. She subsequently served in the post-war French Navy as the *Bouan*.

The *U-532* had been intended to sail for France in early 1944 but had been forced to return short of fuel after both the *Charlotte Schliemann* and the *Brake* had been sunk. She finally left Batavia in January 1945 with a cargo of tin, rubber, wolfram and molybdenum. Junker sank two ships when in the North Atlantic but was still at sea on 4 May when Dönitz called an end to the U-boat war. Junker took the submarine into Liverpool on 10 May to surrender.[9]

The *U-181* left Batavia for Germany in October 1944, carrying the obligatory cargo of strategic materials, and sank the American merchant ship *Fort Lee* as she crossed the Indian Ocean. However, off the Cape the *U-181* developed serious problems with the main bearings on the propeller shafts. There was still 10,000 miles to go, leaving Freiwald with no alternative but to turn back to Batavia, which he reached on 6 January 1945. Since the submarine was returning with a surplus of fuel, arrangements were made for the *U-181* to meet with the *U-843* (*Kapitänleutnant* Oskar Herwartz) and transfer as much fuel as could be spared. The *U-843* eventually reached Bergen but was sunk by air attack in the Kattegat while on the last leg of her long voyage.

One more submarine left the beleaguered Reich in the final days of the war; with Allied troops already fighting east of the Rhine, the *U-234* (*Kapitänleutnant* Johann Fehler) sailed for the Far East from Kiel on 24 March 1945. The Type XB submarine had been specially modified and had embarked 240 tons of valuable cargo, equipment and specialist drawings. She also had three important passengers; a *Luftwaffe* General who was to be the new Air Attache in Tokyo and two senior technical officers of the I.J.N. Because of a fault with the submarine's radio equipment, Dönitz's order to return to Norway was not received until 8 May, by which time the submarine was in the western Atlantic. Fehler felt that he would get better treatment if he surrendered to the Americans rather than the Canadians or British and so ignored instructions to proceed to Halifax. Not wishing to be included in the surrender of the submarine, the two Japanese officers lay in their bunks and took an overdose of luminal; they were buried at sea with full honours. Fehler eventually surrendered to the American destroyer *Sutton* and the submarine was escorted into the Naval Yard at Kittery in Maine.

The Americans found, stowed in the submarine's mine tubes, containers with over 30 tons of mercury, an essential requirement for Japan's munitions programme. Of greater interest to the Americans, and a fact that was kept secret for many years, was a consignment of 78 tons of radioactive uranium oxide – an ingredient for Japan's nuclear weapons programme. At that stage of the war it was obviously impossible for the Germans to have produced such a weapon, but there was still a chance that their allies may have been able to do so. Fate decided otherwise. It was the American bombs dropped on Hiroshima and Nagasaki that ended the war.

The *U-181* was in Singapore, preparing for another attempt at the long trip home, during the final weeks before Germany surrendered. One of the measures being undertaken was the construction of a home-made *schnorkel*, using plans brought out from Germany and based on the one fitted in the *U-1062*. The crew heard the news from home with growing concern as the Russians advanced ever deeper into Germany and surrounded Berlin. They heard the report of the death of Hitler on 3 May and were gravely shaken. They already knew that if the codeword *Lübeck* was received then the submarines were to be handed over to the Japanese. The option of continuing the fight themselves under Japanese command was not considered.

There were six submarines still in ports in Japanese held areas when news of the German surrender was eventually received: the *U-181* and *U-862* were at Singapore, the *U-219* at Batavia, the *U-195* at Surabaya and the two ex-Italian boats *UIT-24* and *UIT-25* were at Kobe in Japan. The procedure for all six was similar. The Japanese arrived at the jetty alongside the German boats. The crews were then instructed to leave immediately and, after the German colours had been lowered, the crews were driven away to nearby camps. The boats were then commissioned into the Japanese Navy, the Germans initially being required to return to maintain the submarines and instruct Japanese crews in their use. None of the boats became operational under the flag of the I.J.N. The two Italian boats thus had the dubious distinction of serving under the flags of all three Axis nations. For the remainder of the war the German crews were left to their own devices but were not allowed to leave their camps. They received none of the inhumane treatment which was meted out to the Italian crews in 1943 or to Allied POWs.

As time went by, the approach of the end of the war became increasingly obvious to the Germans. They could see more and more Allied aircraft flying to raid Singapore, they heard of the dropping of the atomic bombs on Japan, and they were informed of the Japanese surrender. In Malaya they became aware of Chinese guerrilla attacks on Japanese outposts. As Freiwald and Dommes tried to collect all their men into a central camp, several Germans were killed and others wounded when the trains in which they were travelling were attacked. With the arrival of the British they were left alone for several days, as it seems that the presence of these men was unknown to the occupying force. Eventually they ended up in Changi, where they remained from mid-October 1945 until the end of June 1946. Only then did they board the *Empress of Australia* for passage to England. Repatriation to Germany did not begin until 1947, some of the crewmen not arriving back in their homeland until the end of the year.

Statistically, the operations of the German and Italian submarines in the Indian Ocean cannot be considered a resounding success. Of the seven Italian boats converted to cargo carriers, three were sunk on passage out to the Far East, while the machinery of a fourth was such as to make her unreliable. Just three arrived safely. Of these, one was sunk after leaving Penang for the return to France, another sailed but had to return to Penang with defective engines and the third eventually went to Japan for a full overhaul and never became operational again.

In addition to these, sixty-six German and two Italian submarines were deployed operationally, some more than once. This number includes those that were used in Groups such as *Eisbär* or *Seehund*, which only operated in the southern Indian Ocean before returning direct to France. In all, thirty-nine U-boats and one Italian submarine were lost to attacks by Allied anti-submarine patrols either in transit or while in Far East waters. Only two U-boats returned home with a cargo for the German war effort, two more reaching home only to become involved in the German surrender. In addition there had been the enormous administrative effort to keep the boats resupplied and at sea. On the credit side, it demonstrated a willingness to be seen to co-operate with Germany's Asian ally. With the Allied anti-submarine measures making the Atlantic a hostile environment for U-boats, the Indian Ocean was seen as an area where they could still make an impact. Over 150 Allied merchant ships were sunk, totalling nearly a million tons gross. In the event, this confrontation in the Indian Ocean between Germany and the Allies was no war winning battle like that in the Atlantic, yet it served to divert resources, particularly aircraft, that could have been used elsewhere to devastating effect.

Notes:

1 The *Archimede* and the *Leonardo da Vinci*.

2 The codename was changed to *Merkator* after the Italian surrender. The eighth submarine due for conversion, the *Ammiraglio Cagni*, was at sea on patrol off South Africa and surrendered to the British and it was considered that the codename *Aquila* was compromised.

3. The story is told by *Commandante* Auconi in the periodical journal of the 'Sharkhunters', an American based group of submarine enthusiasts.

4 *Haie im Paradies* by Jochen Brennecke, Wilhelm Heyne 1983.

5 The author has been unable to substantiate a report that a few of the reserve stock of American torpedoes captured in the Philipinnes in 1942 were handed over by the Japanese and modified for use by the Germans.

6 Quoted from *Stalin's Silver* by John Beasant, Bloomsbury 1995.

7 *ibid*.

8 The only officer to survive the sinking was the Engineer Officer, *Oberleutnant* Horst Klatt, his story is told in full in *Stalin's Silver*.

9 Junker's War Diary ('KTB' or *Kriegstagebuch*) was confiscated by the two officers who accepted the submarine's surrender – it has not been seen since.

EPILOGUE

The two atomic bombs dropped on Japanese cities brought the Second World War to a close. Many thousands of servicemen, both Allied and Axis, had to be shipped home. Germans and Japanese faced a return to their respective countries to find their homelands destroyed. Many found that on their return they had no homes or families. The submarines returned home too, or were taken out to sea and scuttled by the victors.

The war in the Indian Ocean had been a submariners' war. There had been no great clashes of surface fleets; the ships had been deployed to find and hunt submarines. The aircraft had also been used in an anti-submarine role, spending countless hours seeking an elusive and often hidden enemy. It had been the submariners of the various nations who had borne the brunt of this predominantly naval war.

The submarines would return. During the Cold War the Americans and Russians would criss-cross the ocean, each trying to keep track of the other. The Indonesians would acquire submarines from the Russians in attempts to bolster their power base in the area. Occasionally the British would include submarines in their Far East Fleet. The Indians and the Pakistanis would each add submarines to their own navies to maintain a balance with the other – and from time to time would use them operationally. The Australians would also have submarines. The Iranians too.

The submarines may be different. Little else changes.

Appendix I

Comparison Of Some Naval Ranks

Royal Navy	Other Navies
Sub Lieutenant	Leutnant zur See (Ger)
	Ensign (USA)
Lieutenant (Junior)	Enseigne (Fr)
	Oberleutnant zur See (Ger)
	Tenente di Vascello (It)
	Lieutenant (JG) (USA)
Lieutenant (Senior)	Lieutenant de Vaisseau (Fr)
	Kapitänleutnant (Ger)
	Tenente di Vascello (It)
	Lieutenant (USA)
Lieutenant Commander	Capitaine de Corvette (Fr)
	Korvettenkapitän (Ger)
	Capitano di Corvetta (It)
	Lieutenant Commander (USA)
Commander	Capitaine de Fregate (Fr)
	Fregattenkapitän (Ger)
	Capitano di Fregata (It)
	Commander (USA)
Captain	Capitaine de Vaisseau (Fr)
	Kapitän zur See (Ger)
	Capitano di Vascello (It)
	Captain (USA)

Netherlands:
British equivalent ranks are used in the text, see Chapter Four note 4.
Japan:
British equivalent ranks are used in the text, see Chapter Five note 2.

Appendix II

Characteristics of Typical Submarines

British 'S' Class

Displacement: 814/990 tons
Speed: 14/9 knots
Range: 3,750nm at 10 knots (surface)
Armament: Seven 21 inch torpedo tubes (six forward, one aft)
                 13 torpedoes
                 One 3 inch gun (4 inch in some later boats)
Diving Depth: 350 feet
Complement: 36

British 'T' Class

Displacement: 1,090/1,575 tons
Speed: 15/9 knots
Range   11,000nm at 10 knots (surface)
Armament: Eleven 21 inch torpedo tubes (eight forward, three aft)
                 17 torpedoes
                 One 4 inch gun
Diving Depth: 350 feet
Complement: 65

Dutch K XIV Class

Displacement: 771/1,000 tons
Speed: 17/9 knots
Range: 3,500nm at 11 knots (surface)
Armament: Eight 21 inch torpedo tubes (four forward, two aft and two
                 external amidships). 14 torpedoes
                 One 88mm gun
Diving Depth: 300 feet
Complement: 38

Dutch O 21 Class

Displacement:	881/1,186 tons
Speed:	19.5/9 knots
Range:	8,000nm at 11 knots
Armament:	Eight 21 inch torpedo tubes (Four forward, two aft and two external amidships). 14 torpedoes
	One 88mm gun
Diving Depth	330 feet
Complement:	55

French 1,500 Tonnes Class

Displacement:	1,570/2,084 tons
Speed:	17/10 knots. (Later units had surface speed of 19 or 20 knots)
Range	10,000nm at 10 knots, or 4,000 nm at 17 knots
Armament:	Eleven torpedo tubes (Four 21 inch forward, and two sets of traversing mounts with 21 inch and 15.7 inch external tubes
	One 100mm gun
Diving Depth:	250 feet
Complement:	64

German Type IXC

Displacement:	1,120/1,232 tonnes
Speed:	18.3/7.3 knots
Range:	13,450nm at 10 knots
Armament:	Six 53.3cm (21 inch) torpedo tubes (four forward, two aft). 22 torpedoes
	One 105mm gun (110 rounds), one 37mm and one 20mm
Diving Depth:	100 metres (Crush depth 200 metres)
Complement:	48 (nominal – figure varied in practice)

German Type IXD$_2$

Displacement:	1,616/1,804 tonnes
Speed:	19.2/7 knots
Range:	31,500nm at 10 knots
Armament:	Six 53.3cm torpedo tubes (four forward, two aft) 24 torpedoes
	One 105mm gun (150 rounds), one 37mm and one 20mm
Diving Depth:	100 metres (Crush depth 200 metres)
Complement:	55 (nominal)

German Type XB
Displacement:	1,763/2,177 tonnes
Speed:	16.4/7 knots
Range:	18,450nm at 10 knots
Armament:	Two 53.3cm torpedo tubes aft, 15 torpedoes
	12 mine shafts each side of hull amidships and 6
	forward shafts, 66 mines. (Shafts could be used for
	cargo)
	One 105mm gun.
Complement:	53

Italian *Perla* Class
Displacement:	700/860 tons
Speed:	14/7 knots
Range:	2,500nm at 12 knots or 5,200nm at 8 knots
Armament:	Six 53.3cm (21 inch) torpedo tubes (four forward two
	aft). 14 torpedoes
	One 100mm gun
Diving Depth:	250 feet
Complement:	45

Italian *Guglielmotti* Class

Displacement:	1,016/1,266 tons
Speed:	$17\frac{1}{2}/8$ knots
Range:	9,000nm at 8 knots
Armament:	Eight 53.3cm (21 inch) torpedo tubes (four forward
	four aft). 14 torpedoes
	One 100 mm gun
Diving Depth:	288 feet
Complement:	54

Japanese I-15 Class (as I-30)
Displacement:	2,198/3,654 tons
Speed:	$23\frac{1}{2}/8$ knots
Range:	14,000nm at 16 knots
Armament:	Six 21 inch torpedo tubes (bow). 17 torpedoes
	One 5.5 inch gun, two 25mm
	One floatplane
Diving Depth:	330 feet
Complement:	94

Japanese I-16 Class

Displacement:	2,184/2,554 tons
Speed:	$23\frac{1}{2}$/8 knots
Range:	14,000nm at 16 knots
Armament:	Eight 21 inch torpedo tubes (bow). 20 torpedoes
	One 5.5 inch gun, two 25mm
	Could carry up to three *kaiten*
Diving Depth:	330 feet
Complement:	95

Japanese RO-109 Class

Displacement:	525/601 tons
Speed:	14/7 knots
Range:	3,500nm at 12 knots
Armament:	Four 21 inch torpedo tubes (bow). 8 torpedoes
	One 3 inch gun
Diving Depth:	245 feet
Complement:	38

US *Tambor* Class (as *Grenadier*)

Displacement:	1,475/2,370 tons
Speed:	20/8$\frac{1}{2}$ knots
Range:	11,000nm at 10 knots
Armament:	Ten 21 inch torpedo tubes (six bow four aft). 24 torpedoes
	One 3 inch gun
Diving Depth:	250 feet
Complement:	60

Appendix III

Summary of British Submarine Minelaying by Ceylon Based Submarines

Date	Submarine	No. of Mines	Position
14 Mar 44	*Trespasser*	12	Malacca Strait
19 Mar 44	*Taurus*	12	Aroa islands
18 Apr 44	*Taurus*	12	Penang Approaches
13 May 44	*Surf*	8	Pulo Terutau
14 May 44	*Tally Ho*	12	Malacca Strait
16 May 44	*Tactician*	12	Pulo Terutau
18 May 44	*Sea Rover*	8	Sembilan Islands
2 Jun 44	*Tantulus*	12	Sembilan Islands
3 Jun 44	*Stoic*	8	Butang Islands
4 Jun 44	*Templar*	12	Sembilan Islands
7 Jun 44	*Tantivy*	12	Sembilan Islands
14 Jun 44	*Surf*	8	Pulo Terutau
24 Jun 44	*Truculent*	12	Malacca Strait
6 to 8 Jul 44	*Porpoise*	56	Deli River, Sumatra
16 Sep 44	*Trenchant*	12	Aru Bay, Sumatra
24 Sep 44	*Tudor*	12	West coast Siam
30 Oct 44	*Tradewind*	12	Mergui Islands
19 Nov 44	*Thorough*	12	Malacca Strait
9 Dec 44	*Porpoise*	50	Penang Approaches
16 Dec 44	*Thule*	12	Pulo Terutau
3 Jan 45	*Rorqual*	50	West coast Siam
3 Jan 45	*Rorqual*	12	West coast Siam
9 Jan 45	*Porpoise*[1]	62	Penang Approaches
17 Jan 45	*Rorqual*	50	Andaman Islands
23 Jan 45	*Rorqual*[2]	12	Andaman Islands

Notes:

1 *Porpoise* was lost after laying this minefield.

2 *Rorqual* joined the submarine flotilla at Fremantle after this operation.

BIBLIOGRAPHY

Unpublished Works

Naval Staff History Second World War, Submarines Volume III, Admiralty 1956 (Held in the PRO under reference ADM234/382).
Naval Staff History Second World War, British Mining Operations, MOD 1973.
Monthly Anti-Submarine Reports, issued by the Admiralty, September 1939 to December 1945. (ADM199/2057 et seq.)
Report on Special Operations carried out by HMNethS *O 24* (DEF2/891).
De Koninklijke Marine in de Tweede Wereld-Oorlog, Bureau Maritieme Historie Marinestaf, Den Haag 1958.
German Naval History Series, The U-boat War Volume II January 1942 – May 1943 Admiralty 1952. (ADM234/68)
German U-boat Commanders' War Diaries (KTB – *Kriegstagebuch*) copies held by the Naval Historical Branch of the MOD.
Japanese Monograph 102, Submarine Operations December 1941-April 1942, General HQ US Far East Command 1952.
Japanese Monograph 110, Submarine Operations in the Second Phase, Part I April-August 1942, General HQ US Far East Command 1952.
US Naval Technical Mission to Japan, Target Report S-17, Japanese Submarine Operations, US Navy 1946.

Published Works

Alden, John D: *US Submarine Attacks During World War II*, Naval Institute Press (USA), 1989.
Bagnasco, E: *Submarines of World War Two*, Arms and Armour Press 1977.
Banks, Arthur: *Wings of the Dawning*, Images Publishing, 1996.
Blair, C: *Hitler's U-boat War, The Hunted 1942-45*, Random House, 1998.
Boyd, C & Akihiko Yoshida: *The Japanese Submarine Force In World War II*, Airlife Publishing, 1996.
Brennecke, J; *Haie im Paradies*, Wilhelm Heyne, Munich, 1983.
Brown, David: *Warship Losses of World War Two*, Arms and Armour Press, 1990.
Cruikshank, C: *SOE in the Far East*, Oxford University Press, 1983.
Cunningham, R A: *A Submarine at War, HMS* Taurus *1942-44*, published 1992.
Edwards, B: *Blood and Bushido*, Published 1991.
Gibson, John F: *Dark Seas Above*, Blackwood & Sons Ltd., 1947.
Giese, Otto: *Shooting the War*, Leo Cooper 1994.

Groner, Erich: *German Warships 1815-1945, Vol II (Submarines & Minesweepers)*, Conway 1991.

Gunton, Dennis: *The Penang Submarines*, Phoenix Press, Penang, 1970.

Hashimoto, M: *Sunk: The Story of the Japanese Submarine Fleet 1942-45*, Cassell and Company Ltd, 1954.

Huan, Claude: *Les Sous-Marins Francais 1919-45, Marines edition*, Nantes, 1996.

Kemp, Paul: *The T-Class Submarine*, Arms & Armour Press, 1990.

Mackenzie, Sir H: *The Sword of Damocles*, RN Submarine Museum, 1995.

Marder, Arthur: *Old Friends, New Enemies: The Royal Navy and the Imperial Japanese Navy 1936-41*, Clarendon Press, 1981.

Morison, S E: *History of US Naval Operations in World War II, Volume IV, Submarine Actions May 1942*, Conway Maritime Press, 1986.

Padfield, P: *War Beneath the Sea*, John Murray, 1995.

Polmar N & Carpenter D B: Submarines of the Imperial Japanese Navy 1904-45, Conway Maritime Press, 1986.

Rohwer, Jurgen: *Axis Submarine Successes 1939-45*, Patrick Stephens Ltd, 1983.

Rossler, E: *The U-boat*. Arms & Armour Press, 1981.

Thomas, David: *Japan's War at Sea*, Andre Deutsch, 1978.

Trenowden, I: *Operations Most Secret*, Crecy Books, 1994. *The Hunting Submarine*, William Kimber, 1974.

Turner, L et al: *War in the Southern Oceans*, Oxford University Press, 1961.

Tute, Warren: *The Reluctant Enemies*, William Collins, 1990.

Vat, D van der: *The Pacific Campaign*, Hodder & Stoughton, 1992.

Vause, Jordan: Wolf: *U-Boat Commanders in WW II*, Airlife Publishing, 1997.

Warner P, & Sadao Seno: *The Coffin Boats*, Leo Cooper, 1986.

Winton, J: *The Forgotten Fleet*, Michael Joseph Ltd, 1969

Young, Edward: *One of Our Submarines*, Rupert-Hart, 1953. Republished by Wordsworth Editions Ltd. in 1997.

GENERAL INDEX

Note: All officers are indexed under the highest rank attained in this story.
Surface warships, submarines and merchant ships are indexed separately.

INDEX OF SHIP NAMES